# Unshakable
# KIDS

"Brimming with unshakable truth, undeniable research, and unfailing tools, this book will give you the practical help you need to build a firm foundation for your kids to stand on! I appreciate Lauren's simple yet profound Brain Builders and grounding principles in each chapter."

**Amy Seiffert**, author of *Starved*

"Raising Jesus-loving, emotionally healthy kids just got simpler . . . and it all starts with emotionally and spiritually healthy parents. Utilizing her background in psychology, Lauren Gaines delivers clear strategies for transforming stress-filled households into peace-infused homes. She speaks the truth Christian parents need to hear while offering practical tools that will help them succeed."

**Stephanie Gilbert**, author and cohost of
the *Pastors' Wives Tell All* podcast

"*Unshakable Kids* is a book that shook me to my core in the most life-affirming way. Lauren's authenticity shines, creating a heartwarming welcome as she leads the conversation with honesty, courage, and grace. As a pediatric nurse practitioner, I know every mom will be encouraged and inspired by the practical advice Lauren gives for those longest days and shortest years of early mothering. As a professor, I am wildly enthusiastic about the Brain Builders and Faith Formers, practical tools for any stage of parenting. But as a mom of four teens, reading this book made me feel deeply seen and understood as I reflected on my own journey to raise spiritually strong and emotionally healthy children. This book gifts moms with hope and comfort in knowing we are not alone in the God-inspired mission of motherhood."

**Jessica L. Peck**, DNP, APRN, CPNP-PC, CNE, CNL, FAANP,
FAAN, author of *Behind Closed Doors*, past president of
the National Association of Pediatric Nurse Practitioners,
and clinical professor of nursing, Baylor University

"It's pretty cool that I just changed my children's lives with less than twenty dollars. That's not something I get to say very often. *Unshakable Kids* is the handbook I desperately needed yesterday, today, and tomorrow. With a solid biblical foundation, Lauren marries her personal experiences and professional understanding as a school psychologist to provide knowledge and practical tools, undergirded with truth, to foster spiritually and emotionally healthy children. This is a must-read for any parent at any stage of parenthood."

**Rachael H. Elmore**, MA, LCMHC-S, NCC, author of *A Mom Is Born*, owner and director of Elmore Christian Counseling, Nationally Certified Counselor

"Our children are living in a world that is far from steady. I get rocked by the challenges of parenting daily. In *Unshakable Kids*, Lauren powerfully renews your faith toward parenting problems, leaving grace for your mistakes and failures. This book is for anyone who feels hopeless about where our world is headed. Lauren brilliantly walks alongside you as a friend, teaching you how to raise spiritually strong and emotionally healthy children."

**Christy Boulware**, founder and president of Fearless Unite, mental health advocate, speaker, author, and leader

"I love this book! I have the privilege of serving women of all generations, and it excites me when I discover a resource that can help moms raise kind, well-adjusted children. This book is one of those resources. As you take the journey with Lauren in *Unshakable Kids*, you will laugh and say 'ouch,' because we have all had our patience give way to destructive behavior that brings bad results in our children. Take a breath, learn a new way to parent, and apply these biblical principles. Our most significant legacy is our children, and they are worth this investment. By the way, these principles apply to any age—bonus!"

**Liz DeFrain**, Women's Director of the PennDel Ministry Network

# Unshakable KIDS

## THREE KEYS TO RAISING SPIRITUALLY STRONG AND EMOTIONALLY HEALTHY CHILDREN

# LAUREN GAINES

BakerBooks

*a division of Baker Publishing Group*
Grand Rapids, Michigan

Published by Baker Books
a division of Baker Publishing Group
Grand Rapids, Michigan
www.bakerbooks.com

Printed in the United States of America

Library of Congress Cataloging-in-Publication Data
Names: Gaines, Lauren, 1985– author.
Title: Unshakable kids : three keys to raising spiritually strong and emotionally healthy children / Lauren Gaines.
Description: Grand Rapids, Michigan : Baker Books, a division of Baker Publishing Group, [2023] | Includes bibliographical references.
Identifiers: LCCN 2022051575 | ISBN 9781540902450 (paperback) | ISBN 9781540903594 (casebound) | ISBN 9781493443222 (ebook)
Subjects: LCSH: Motherhood—Religious aspects—Christianity. | Mothers—Religious life. | Parenting—Religious aspects—Christianity. | Anxiety—Religious aspects—Christianity.
Classification: LCC BV4529.18 .G34 2023 | DDC 248.8/45—dc23/eng/20230227
LC record available at https://lccn.loc.gov/2022051575

This publication is intended to provide helpful and informative material on the subjects addressed. Readers should consult their personal health professionals before adopting any of the suggestions in this book or drawing inferences from it. The author and publisher expressly disclaim responsibility for any adverse effects arising from the use or application of the information contained in this book.

The author is represented by The FEDD Agency, Inc.

Baker Publishing Group publications use paper produced from sustainable forestry practices and post-consumer waste whenever possible.

23  24  25  26  27  28  29      7  6  5  4  3  2  1

To my Nona, who laid a firm foundation of faith
in my heart at a young age and who showed
me what a joy it is to raise children.

# Contents

# Contents

# Introduction

Wonder filled my journey to motherhood. The anticipation was so captivating, and I dreamt of what life would be like with a baby for over nine months.

After my daughter's birth, as much as I cherished holding my precious child, the sleepless nights, poop explosions, and cluster feedings started to take some of the joy out of the experience. I had no idea motherhood would require so much of me.

As we added more children to the bunch, I started to feel overwhelmed by the reality of caring for children twenty-four hours a day, seven days a week. Motherhood drained me emotionally, physically, and mentally more than I could've ever imagined.

How can something so good be so hard?

One morning I snapped. My intentions started out good as I planned our morning devotions and sipped my lukewarm coffee. We had stayed home from church because my husband had to work for the seventh day straight and one of our kids was sick. Instead of attending church, I planned to be the stand-in Sunday school teacher. My new stickers and stationery boosted my mood as I created a beautiful-looking Bible lesson for my kids. I had no doubt our morning would be filled with abundant praise and divine touches from heaven. Mothers make kids' activities look so easy on Instagram; how hard could it *really* be? We'd have a great time of family worship together at home.

Unfortunately, the morning didn't play out in real life like it had in my head. It started off okay at first. We turned on "Reckless Love," and the kids asked to bring out their instruments. "Sure, that's fine," I said.

"Hey! I had it first. Mommy! He's not giving it back!"

"No, I had it first! Ugh! You *never* share with me." *Stomp. Yell. Roar.*

My grand vision for our morning faded right before my eyes. Desperate, I redirected the kids, "Guys, there are plenty of instruments to play with. We need to take turns. Now, let's sing to Jesus." I closed my eyes, put my hands up in praise, and tried to ignore the tension in our home. But after a few seconds of peace, I heard more screaming and crying.

Without warning, I exploded, "That's it! I've had enough of your fighting. You guys are acting like spoiled brats! Give me that drum. No one is going to play with it if you keep fighting." I snatched the toy out of my daughter's hand, dramatically threw it on the couch, and finished my tirade by screaming, "WE ARE SUPPOSED TO BE PRAISING JESUS!"

All the kids started to cry. As soon as I saw their tears, I felt guilty for losing my cool. Earlier that morning, excitement had coursed through my body. Minutes later, I let my raging emotions burst forth and ruin the mood. What happened? It should've been easy.

Though it wasn't the morning I'd imagined, sadly, it didn't catch me completely off guard. Because if I'm being honest, it wasn't the first time something like this had happened.

### Am I Ruining My Kids?

I used to let my emotions fester until they reached a boiling point and I could no longer control them. Sometimes I'd lose my temper and yell. Other times I'd anxiously pace the house wondering what I should do next. Sometimes my kids provoked my frustration. Other times my unease came from the world feeling too dark and heavy.

Either way, I'd find myself lying awake at night staring at the ceiling and asking, *Am I ruining my kids? What if I'm doing it all wrong?* My job as their parent was to nurture and guide their little hearts, but I often felt unprepared to complete the assignment. What if I accidentally crushed them instead?

Parenting left me feeling flustered. There were so many decisions to make. What if I made the wrong one? Many nights I worried I'd made a mistake that day and hurt my child's chances of having a good life. My heart longed to give my kids good childhoods, ones they didn't have to recover from as adults. But in the everyday moments, my thoughts spiraled, and I'd react to stressful situations in unhealthy ways.

As a parent, I expected my kids to be respectful, grounded, and mentally balanced, yet my behaviors often taught them the opposite. Parenting exhausted me emotionally, and it often showed in my actions.

If I had such a hard time remaining levelheaded, how did I expect to raise children with sound minds who remained in control of their emotions? I hoped to give my children the tools to verbally, not physically, share their feelings, yet I wasn't sure exactly how to do that. I was lucky if I could get the kids out the door with everything they needed for school that day. Forget trying to raise a child who loves Jesus and is respectful, confident, and kind.

As I opened up to my friends about my experiences in motherhood, I quickly realized I wasn't the only parent who felt uncertain about exactly *how* to raise good, strong kids. As I walked with other moms in our neighborhood and talked with fellow moms in person and online, I noticed many similarities. We all wanted to be emotionally balanced women who felt confident in our parenting, but every time the earth trembled, we started shaking too. We shook because we believed the lie that we could never be good enough parents or the world was too ugly to raise a godly, loving child in it. We felt anxious about the emotional health of our kids and stressed over *how* to raise spiritually strong children who wouldn't compromise to sin.

There had to be another way. I wasn't satisfied with worrying about my kids all the time. I had to make a choice: I could either stay stuck in my frustration or I could take action. I chose to do something about it because I realized if I didn't take up the responsibility to mold my kids' impressionable minds, someone or something else would. And I didn't like that option at all.

If you don't like the idea of sitting back and hoping for the best, this book is for you. You can parent with a sound mind and confidence. I know this because I spent years figuring out how to do it.


## A Better Way

Before kids, I worked as a school psychologist in Baltimore City Public Schools. Every day I taught my students how to be mentally tough and cope with the stress of life. When I made the choice to find a better way to live and parent my kids, I reread all my textbooks from graduate school on human development and psychology. I spent hours researching the best parenting methods and discovering concrete strategies to help me build a firm foundation in my children. I found it was possible to raise emotionally healthy children who understood the power of the mind. My kids could learn to stand strong and live uncompromised lives in a world filled with compromise.

With God's help, I found a better way to parent. And in *Unshakable Kids*, I share the path forward with you. You, too, can go from meltdown mama to peaceful parent. The foundation you lay for your children will change their lives forever. Change is possible for you and your family. You can raise God-fearing children who, using their heavenly perspectives, are able to spot the lies of the enemy. You can decide right now to intentionally train your children to flourish in a broken world.

Though I must warn you, the change may not come overnight. For me, at times, the progress felt slow—a little too slow. But as I embraced the resistance, I discovered key principles to help us thrive together as a family.

I no longer felt stuck in my frazzled, accidental parenting methods. The struggles still came, but I now had a plan and felt like it was possible to parent without losing my mind. The three key growth areas I discovered can help focus your parenting too. You can intentionally raise children who won't get flustered with every challenge they face and who can successfully handle life's stress using their toolbox of healthy coping strategies.

## Made to Mother

Part of parenting with bravery and boldness is completely trusting God's plan for your family. Right now, you're going to throw all the doubts and fears out the window, including the voices that tell you you've made too many mistakes already or you're a lost cause because you weren't taught emotional health growing up. Those voices must go.

Will you make mistakes? Of course. There's no such thing as a perfect parent. But what if God put you and me in this generation for a specific reason? What if we were born to raise kids in such a time as this?

God gave *you* your children for a reason. Don't believe God is that deliberate? Look around you. God carefully and intentionally created our world. The majestic waterfalls, snowcapped mountaintops, and large blooming dahlias were not created by accident. The miracle of a child being formed in a mother's womb doesn't happen by chance. If God is so purposeful about making every flower, animal, fruit, and beach, then surely He didn't make a mistake when He gave you your unique children. You were made to mother in this moment. And God intentionally created your children to be raised by a mother like you.

Parenting with purpose isn't about controlling our children's lives or never making mistakes as parents. It's about trusting the God of the universe and believing He gave us our kids to raise in this exact moment in time.

## What to Expect

*Unshakable Kids* will give you the tools to raise kids with well-balanced minds who are confident and filled with self-control.

In part 1, we'll dive deep into the three foundational areas: our children's minds, hearts, and identities. To raise emotionally and spiritually healthy kids, we need to intentionally cultivate these three areas. Through the first section, we'll discover how to overcome unhelpful mindsets and encourage healthy neural connections in our children's minds. We'll find the best ways to win the hearts of our children and nourish strong, healthy identities in them.

In part 2, we'll take an inventory of our homes and learn how to build life-giving places that support the growth of positive neural connections in our children's brains. With whole minds and hearts, we'll uncover the best way to support healthy spiritual and emotional growth in our day-to-day lives.

Part of the learning process includes completing Brain Builder and Faith Former activities. Throughout the chapters, you'll find challenges and tasks to guide you as you lay solid foundations in your children's lives. These tools were intentionally designed to help you overcome mental mistakes, heal any lingering heart wounds, and strengthen your walk with Jesus.

Change often requires action. To get the most out of this book, set aside time to complete the tasks. This will encourage you to help your children win the battle of the mind and live victori-ously. As you read, mark up the pages, write in the margins, and highlight phrases that stick out to you. Make sure you take time to digest and reflect on what you read. Emotional and spiri-tual growth doesn't happen overnight, but you can shape your children's minds, hearts, and identities with time and intention, helping them become the people God destined them to be.

# 1

# The Mental Game of Motherhood

One night when our oldest daughter was in kindergarten, all my exhaustion, anger, and frustration compounded into one awful, hard day.

I was in the kitchen chopping vegetables and encouraging our daughter to try her best when our son came running in screaming, "Adelyn just ate the kinetic sand!"

"WHAT!? Why is the kinetic sand even out?" I yelled. As I quickly googled the risks associated with a one-year-old eating kinetic sand, I altogether lost it. I tore through the house, dramatically throwing the kinetic sand in the garbage and screaming at my children as the kitchen timer beeped in the background.

I had grown so tired of the mess. Tired of being pulled in a million different directions at the same time. Tired of the stuff. EVERYWHERE. Tired of feeling like I bore the weight of life by myself.

My mind spiraled downward, and nothing could stop the decline.

I thought to myself, *This is too much. Raising kids is exhausting, and I don't want to do it anymore. The house is always a mess, I can't catch a break, and the continual chaos in our home is making me anxious. Is life always going to be this hard?*

One more loud scream from my kids running through the kitchen was all it took for me to lose my cool. Suddenly I found myself releasing all the hurts and frustrations of the day.

"I'm tired of this mess! I'm always the one who has to clean up, and it's not fair. Stop acting so wild and start acting more responsible!"

My cutting words revealed my frustration boiling on the inside. I was overwhelmed and tired. The chaos had brought it all to the surface. As the joy was sucked right out of me, I started to feel guilty for yelling at my children. They were just being kids and hadn't intentionally done anything wrong. Yet I'd taken my frustration out on them because my thoughts weren't healthy.

Each challenging day brought a new self-defeating thought to fight against: *I'm not doing enough as a mom. I'm trying my best every day, yet I can't seem to stay on top of the housework. The constant whining and moaning from my kids must mean I'm doing something wrong.* My negative beliefs quickly turned into negative words, and the cycle of feeling frazzled in motherhood lived on. But one day as I read about the brain and how it shapes our thoughts and actions, God showed me something unexpected.

## Here's the Truth

You bought this book hoping it would help your child, but here's the truth: to raise emotionally healthy children, we mamas need to focus on our emotional health first. I didn't realize how much my brain needed transforming until I started to research ways to help my children build their emotional health.

We can tell our kids to be strong until we're blue in the face, but actions speak louder than words, *right*? It's kind of scary how quickly we, as parents, can become trapped in downward mental spirals. The negative thoughts are automatic, and the smallest inconveniences push us over the edge. We linger on questions about the future, we aren't confident in our decision-making skills, and we harp on everything we do wrong.

We quickly lose our temper more often than we'd like to admit, and our minds are overwhelmed by the thought that maybe we aren't parenting the "right" way. We want our children to be mentally tough, but what we really need is to learn how to control our *own* thoughts. How can we possibly raise worry-free kids when we feel anxious and frustrated every day?

We want to put on a brave face and show the world we have it all together as parents, but we know the truth: behind the scenes, we feel ill-equipped and emotionally exhausted. We slip into telling ourselves, *One day parenting won't be so hard.* But as each day of parenthood presents new challenges, we can't fathom how we'll get there. Something needs to change, but we don't know what or how. We "tried" harder, and it didn't work.

This is what I know: there's a battle raging in not only our children's minds but our minds too. In the mental game of motherhood, we're losing.

The good news is, no matter how draining parenting can be, there's still hope. Together, you and I can help our children develop healthy thinking patterns and strong neural pathways. It won't be easy, and you're probably going to face some doubts along the way, but don't let that stop you from finding a breakthrough. You can parent with confidence and clarity. Even in the midst of a storm, you can feel peace as a parent. When you prioritize your emotional and mental health, you're helping not only yourself but also your kids.

Lasting change in your family starts with you.

Let's stop blaming our circumstances for our instability and start fighting the true enemy. The devil doesn't want us to know that when we take every thought captive, we free not only ourselves but also our children and our children's children.

Friend, we must fight for our sound minds. Not just for our own sanity, but for generations to come. The fight is worth it! When our minds are in check, we can raise kids who know exactly who they are and whose they are—children of God.

## A Brain Can Be Retrained

Part of our journey together includes retraining our brains. We used to be taught that once a brain is formed, it cannot be altered. But new research shows you *can* in fact change the physical structure of your brain. It's called neuroplasticity. So even if your brain is systemically designed to think a negative thought, it doesn't have to stay that way forever. You can reshape negative neural pathways.

How? By thinking new thoughts. *New York Times* bestselling author Jennie Allen puts it this way: "When we think new thoughts, we physically alter our brains. When we think new thoughts, we make healthier neural connections. When we think new thoughts, we blaze new trails. When we think new thoughts, everything changes for us."[1]

You can create new mental habits. New pathways are straight ahead. Are you ready for everything to change?

Maybe in the past you weren't intentional about your thought life or maybe you've made some mistakes in developing your child's social and emotional health. Please hear this: it's never too late. New neural pathways are built each day, and old habits, thoughts, and hurts can be replaced with new patterns and beliefs. A brain can be retrained.

In this journey, you may need to face some ugly thoughts. You may also notice that some of your habits and rhythms may need to change. Change isn't always fun, but it's better than staying stuck. You don't need to stay immobilized in your toxic thoughts. Your thoughts *can* be transformed.

Do you think God knew our brains were capable of change when He created us? I like to think He did. In Romans 12:2, we're given specific insight into this internal change when Paul writes,

> Do not be conformed to this world (this age), [fashioned after and adapted to its external, superficial customs], but be transformed (changed) by the [entire] renewal of your mind [by its new ideals and its new attitude], so that you may prove [for yourselves] what is the good and acceptable and perfect will of God, even the thing which is good and acceptable and perfect [in His sight for you]. (AMPC)

Being transformed by the renewal of our minds demonstrates that our brains can make literal changes in the forms or formulas of thought.[2] Old thought patterns no longer define us. Past mistakes or present pessimistic thoughts no longer bind us. We have the power to change how our brains think, and that's significant because our mental meditation influences our families every day.

Does that mean we should ignore our past mistakes? No. It can be helpful to process the hurts, hang-ups, and mistakes of old. But our past or current struggles shouldn't define everything about our future. It doesn't matter if we weren't intentional in our parenting previously or if we've started to pass down irrational fears to our kids.

God created us with the ability to change. God not only offers us complete transformation, but He also freely gives us new mercies every morning (Lam. 3:22–23). That means even if we get it completely wrong as parents, God is quick to offer His compassion. God's mercy frees us from any guilt or punishment we may deserve. How awesome that even in our failure, God freely shares His loving-kindness with us.

Not too long ago, I experienced God's transforming power firsthand.

"Hurry up! Get your shoes on. I don't want to tell you again. We need to leave or we're going to be late," I yelled at my kids for the third time. It was 7:28 a.m., and we needed to be out of the house and on the road by 7:30.

Everyone finally had their shoes on and we rushed out the door. While I struggled to get my crying baby buckled into her car seat, my oldest child said, "Oops, Mom. I forgot my jacket. Can you help me find it?" I glanced at my watch. *Yup, we're definitely going to be late.* As we finally drove down the road, my heart ached, and I told myself, *We can't keep doing this every morning.*

Later that night I stood in the kitchen, tears rolling down my face as I told my husband, "I can't do this anymore. It's too hard. I'm too tired, and I can't imagine doing this for the rest of the school year. Darryl, I'm not going to make it."

My heart felt discouraged and my mind overwhelmed.

Thankfully, my sweet husband recognized that my thoughts were spiraling downward and said, "Lauren, I don't want you to be upset the whole school year, but I believe God can turn this situation around. Let's pray about it and see what we can do to make it easier for you."

Our oldest daughter had just started kindergarten, and every morning we needed to be out of the house by 7:30 to drive thirty minutes to her school. That meant every morning I needed to wake up, eat breakfast, get three kids dressed and ready, and nurse our baby all before 7:30.

I know that for some people, waking up that early doesn't seem too bad, but I love my sleep, and waking up before 6:00 a.m. feels unnatural to me. Waking up early and rushing everyone out the door without losing my mind felt impossible.

My husband gave me a big hug as I continued to hold back tears, and he said, "Let's pray right now."

"God, in Your Word, You said Your grace is sufficient. That means it is enough for Lauren today. Your strength is made perfect in our weakness. God, give her the strength to do what she needs to do for our family and give her joy as she does it. In Jesus's name, amen."

To my amazement, in the weeks that followed, God brought peace to my overwhelmed mind and heart. Before I knew it, I no longer dreaded our morning routine.

God rewired my thoughts after I gave my mental meditations over to Him. As my husband and I prayed each morning, God transformed my perspective and made sure I didn't lose hope.

When I think back to the situation, I'm amazed by how my mind changed. I looked forward to the time with my children. God rewired my brain and changed my thoughts from "Driving my kids to school is a burden I don't want to bear" to "What a blessing it is to spend one-on-one time with my children each day in the car."

The quality time we spent together in the car will never be forgotten. We sang, laughed, and made memories we wouldn't have made if I had given up right away and never asked God for help.

When I first faced the challenge, I focused on the impossibility of the task before me. I tried to do it in my own strength, and I failed. Thankfully, God intervened before my negative thinking patterns could hinder my heart.

Now, I understand there will be times when we pray or try harder and our situation still doesn't change. It's okay to pivot if whatever we're doing just isn't working. In these situations, we need to ask God for wisdom and then follow His leading.

But if He encourages us to keep pushing forward, then we need to remember this: No matter what the challenge is, God is capable of transforming any negative thoughts we have related to it. He can change our minds.

God designed our brains to be flexible and malleable. That night as I cried in the kitchen to my husband, I didn't have one positive thought about waking up early and driving my kids to school. If I continued, I'd lose my mind, that was all I was certain of. But God had other plans. Through prayer and surrender,

God showed up and changed my hopeless thoughts to optimistic beliefs.

If you feel stuck in negative thought patterns or unhelpful beliefs, God can transform your mind too. You don't need to stay stuck in worry, fear, hopelessness, or discouragement. With the help of the Holy Spirit, you can leave behind your overwhelmed mind and instead take hold of a sound mind—one without worrying, questioning, or complaining. You can parent with intentionality and peace, not because your circumstances have changed but because your mind has been renewed.

Breakthroughs in parenting come when you understand that peace and confidence aren't contingent on your circumstances. Peace doesn't come from an absence of trial. It comes by making a conscious decision to take captive our thoughts each day. The moment you realize you're the one who holds the power to claim what you think about, the direction of your life changes.

If you can't seem to control your negative thoughts, don't panic. That's the first key principle we tackle in this book. When I took a step back and analyzed my own thought patterns, I realized many of them weren't helpful or even rational. My mental game was weak, but thankfully God's grace isn't dependent on our strength.

We don't have to live life on the edge. Our doubts and fears can be replaced by God's peace when we put our hope and trust in Him. We can control our minds instead of allowing our minds to control us. We can parent with confidence.

Get off the starting block today, friend. Take that first step. Push forward even when it feels uncomfortable. Find the time in your busy schedule to dig deep. Trust me, I've seen the reward— and you don't want to miss it.

# 2

# The Three Key Growth Areas

The other day I pushed our two-year-old in the stroller as we walked through our neighborhood. We didn't have a lot of time, but I knew it would be good for our souls to get out and breathe some fresh air. The cold weather was rapidly approaching in Pennsylvania, and there wouldn't be many more nice days to go for a walk outside. I buckled her into the stroller, gave her a granola bar to eat, started the timer on my fitness app, and went off down the road.

Our walk started off peaceful at first. Beautiful blue skies and crisp, cool air greeted us on a perfect fall day. The vibrant leaves seemed to dance off the trees in the most whimsical ways. But five minutes in, my daughter's snack had disappeared, and she began persistently asking to get out of the stroller to walk by herself. In the past, I'd let her run around a cul-de-sac in our neighborhood halfway through our normal route. And a toddler never forgets!

I told her once we got to the cul-de-sac, she could run around for a bit. Well, my answer didn't satisfy her, and as a result, she started screaming at the top of her lungs. In our quiet neighborhood, I seriously felt like her screams echoed off the houses. I tried to walk faster to get to the cul-de-sac, frantically turning on Daniel Tiger music while telling her, "We're almost there. Please be patient." My best attempts to soothe her big feelings did nothing to stop her screams. She was mad, and she wanted the world to know it. After a minute of screaming, I told her, "You know what? Even when we get to the cul-de-sac, I won't let you out of the stroller because you are not behaving."

Then I told myself, *Try to ignore her. Maybe in a few minutes, she'll stop crying.* She didn't stop. Eventually, I'd had enough, so I turned around and started to jog back to our house as fast as I could. At this point, I wanted to address her misbehavior privately. As I ran, I hoped none of the neighbors witnessed our train wreck of a walk.

Wouldn't you know, at the end of our street, I saw our neighbor walking her two dogs. As we got closer, my daughter magically stopped crying. *Thank you, Jesus.* And she said, "Ohhh, look, Mommy! Doggies!"

My first reaction was to laugh. *Really, kid? That's what's going to make you stop crying?* I shared with my neighbor how my hope of having a peaceful walk had gotten squashed by a two-year-old. Thankfully, as a fellow mom, she could relate to my struggle. After we joked for a few minutes about how crazy kids can be, I took my toddler inside to address what had happened.

As I talked with her, I tried to be mindful of her feelings. Getting out of the stroller brings her such joy, and I knew she'd wanted to walk by herself. No mom likes seeing her child upset, but that day I'd hoped to get some exercise, and she needed to learn that if mommy says "no" or "not right now," it's not okay to throw a huge fit. Is it all right to be frustrated? Of course. As humans, all of us experience negative emotions from time to time. Frustration is a natural response to not getting our way. But that doesn't make it okay to scream the entire time because we feel upset.

Have you ever experienced one of those moments when you wanted to be mindful of your child's feelings but you also needed to address a crossed boundary? On that day, my toddler had to learn that her reaction to her frustration wasn't appropriate and she could learn better ways to manage her big feelings.

In the past, I may have lost my cool during that walk. I probably would've yelled and said things I'd later regret in hopes that it would make my toddler comply. The trouble with that is she'd end up focusing on my anger instead of her misbehavior. Then we'd both get mad and find ourselves sucked into a downward spiral of annoyance.

In those chaotic moments of motherhood, it's helpful to have a plan for handling our children's strong feelings. Instead of allowing their negative emotions to ruin our day, we can respond intentionally to build their emotional health.

## The Reward of Intentionality

If we want to equip our children to stand strong and face adversity head-on, we need to look at what's feeding their current behavior. Whether or not we realize it, the world our children engage in influences their behavior daily. The things my kids have learned from TV alone are astonishing. When my son was two years old, he began "grring" like Daniel Tiger when he felt frustrated. My daughter often acted out scenes from her favorite movies long after watching them. And my sister learned how to tie her shoes by herself, not from my parents, but from watching *Sesame Street*.

Though these are lighthearted examples, they demonstrate how much our children absorb from the things they see, hear, and experience every day. Children are great imitators, and it starts early. Babies as young as six months old learn to copy the people around them. And they don't just copy their parents. Scientists found six-month-old babies will engage in imitation games with strangers.[1] It's amazing that a child will mimic some-one they don't even know at such a young age. But it makes sense, because imitation is how young infants learn cultural norms and routines.

We all learn from one another, and we have an innate drive to copy one another's behaviors, thoughts, feelings, and actions. At two years old, a little girl sees her best friend wearing her hair up in a ponytail, and then she starts insisting she wear her hair the same way. A little boy watches another child on the playground hit his brother, so the next day he decides to hit his sibling at home to see what happens. A three-year-old hears a cuss word at the grocery store, and now he's shouting it as loud as he can from the shopping cart.

Everyone, including adults, mimics and copies other people's behavior. It may be something small like using the exact phrases our friends do in conversation or something big like excluding a girl who dresses oddly from our Bible study because none of our friends like her.

If friends, social media, and the news have the power to influ-ence adults, how much more does information from peer groups, teachers, parents, and movies impact our children? What our children see, hear, and experience daily shapes their impres-sionable young minds.

As their guardians, we need to take a step back every now and then to see what's influencing them. When we pause, we can usually identify the habits they pick up from their friends, family members, or favorite characters.

Recently my daughter reminded me of the power of influence. I hate being late to events, but no matter how hard I try to plan ahead, I still find myself rushing my kids out the door about once a week. In all the chaos, I tend to say or do things I later regret. My youngest reminded me of this while I was driving the other day. We were stuck at a red light, and she screamed from the back, "What are these stupid people doing?"

*Oops,* I thought. Kids listen, observe, and copy everything they see. The real question is, What unintentional habits or characteristics do our kids pick up from us?

We may intend to teach our children skills like self-control, but what happens when we feel rushed and frustrated? What do our actions reinforce to our children? These simple, everyday responses often significantly impact our kids' lives, and we may not even realize it unless we take the time to pause and reflect.

Throughout this book, you'll be given opportunities to uncover any hidden habits, thoughts, or mindsets holding you or your family back from living a full, abundant life. Take advantage of these times of reflection. It takes intentionality to successfully shape our children's lives, and the reward of intentionality is one you don't want to miss.

## Three Key Growth Areas

To parent with purpose, let's look at three key growth areas to focus on when nurturing children: the mind, the heart, and identity. Using these three areas, we can raise children who walk through life with strength, purpose, and a solid understanding of their God-given identities. In this chapter, we'll explore *why* it's important to nourish these three growth areas using a biblical and psychological perspective.

### 1. Nourishing the Mind

When we first become parents, we often worry about how much milk our babies need and if they meet their developmental milestones on time. It's natural to be concerned about such things. However, as I studied human development, I realized the first few years of a child's life are so much more than gaining weight and learning to crawl.

Let's go back to the beginning. Babies are born extremely dependent on external care for survival. They need someone to provide safety, food, love, and nourishment to help them thrive. With time, babies become more independent, but not without massive amounts of physical, cognitive, emotional, and social growth. In just twelve months, a child goes from not being able to lift his head without support to walking, talking, smiling, and coloring independently. As the child grows, the brain rapidly develops, forming new neural pathways each day.

Children's minds are like sponges. Every experience, whether positive or negative, changes the physical shape of their brains. Harvard researchers discovered that more than one million new neural connections form every second during the first few years of a child's life.[2] Let that sink in. Every second! That's an incredible amount of growth! By the age of five, a child's brain is 90 percent formed.[3] Which means most of the brain's infrastructure is built before a child even enters kindergarten. The building blocks for learning and future brain development are set at an early age.

See what I mean about an infant's life being about much more than milk consumption? Those initial neural connections matter. The brain connections built in infancy, toddlerhood, and childhood lay the foundation for their thought patterns, habits, and beliefs for years to come.

So, this begs the question, Are we paying close enough attention to the habits, rhythms, standards, and thoughts being laid in our children's minds when they're young? This is one reason we start with the mind first. It's a foundational part of child development, and we can make an intentional choice to shape it for good. As we study the brain and Scripture, we'll learn practical tools to develop a solid plan to build a strong base in our children's brains and limbic systems during critical developmental periods.

We can intentionally teach our children how to pay attention to their thoughts from a young age, so they won't need to learn how to retrain their brains when they're old. Doing this doesn't mean we try to create a perfect childhood for them. It means we give them the tools to handle adversity, uncomfortable feelings, and seasons of trial early on.

To do this, we need to stop viewing negative feelings as the enemy. They are warning signs, and kids should be allowed to feel them. Judith S. Beck, an American psychologist whose father founded cognitive therapy, writes, "Negative emotions are as much a part of the richness of life as positive emotions and serve as important a function as does physical pain, often alerting us to potential problems we may need to address."[4] Instead of sheltering our kids from every negative emotion, what if we taught them to recognize their bad moods, sleeping difficulties, or meltdowns as warning signals that burnout is straight ahead?

When we teach them the proper skills, kids can pay attention to the warning signs. To do this, they must learn how to silence their minds and take a step back to accurately see what their brains are telling them. And remember what I said about parents needing these skills too? When was the last time you sat still and truly cleared your mind?

Together in the mind section of this book, we'll dive deeper into common mental mistakes people often make. Through a detailed process, you'll learn how to identify lies you believe and how to renounce each lie with a truth from God's Word. That's the first step in practicing peace of mind. As we practice taking our thoughts captive, we'll be better able to teach our children to rewire their brains and grab hold of helpful mindsets.

With the specific strategies in this book, you'll be able to teach your children exactly how to take control of their thoughts first thing in the morning. Understanding our mental battles and teaching our kids to do the same saves a lot of future hurt feelings, frustrations, and arguments, which leads me to the second growth area to focus on nurturing in our children—the heart.

## 2. Nourishing the Heart

Current research supports intentionally shaping our children's minds and hearts when they're young, but so does Scripture. We read in Proverbs 22:6, "Train up a child in the way he should go, And when he is old he will not depart from it." God cares deeply about the condition of our hearts, and He instructs us to do the same for our children by training them when they are young. He desires for us to bring our children into a relationship with Jesus by shepherding their hearts from birth. We can't guarantee our children's salvation, but we can do things when they're small to get them on the right track and help them accurately assess the meditations of their hearts.

We'll start by learning the heart-mind connection in the heart growth area. It's vital we understand this principle because it furthers our emotional and spiritual health. We tend to focus so much on transforming our thoughts that we forget about changing our hearts. The Bible doesn't tell us to only guard our minds. Proverbs 4:23 says,

> Above all else, guard your heart,
> for everything you do flows from it. (NIV)

Our minds are powerful, but where do you think those thoughts come from? The depths of our hearts. Our hearts determine the course of our lives and are the center of it all. Our hearts reveal what the deepest parts of us think, feel, and believe—all of which shape our destiny. If our hearts hold the power to shape our lives, are we paying close enough attention to what's in them? That's why if we want lasting emotional stability, we can't stop at mind renewal; we must push further and inspect the issues of the heart.

Through this growth area, we'll learn how to heal any lingering heart wounds and confront sin in our children's lives. We need healed hearts and renewed minds to become the people God created us to be.

After we deal with our own heart issues, we can discover how to intentionally win our children's hearts. To do this, we'll look at what psychology and the Bible say about effective and healthy parenting. We'll also learn how to build up our children's self-esteem and confidence. Then we'll figure out how to easily apply these parenting principles to our daily lives.

With intentionality, we can learn how to mother joyfully and find special "I love you" moments with our kids throughout the day. The "I love you" moments happen when we are intentionally present and recognize the preciousness of heart-to-heart connection. Moments when we share our favorite part of the day, hug each other for longer than ten seconds, or put the phone down and chat while looking our children in the eyes. Together we'll discover how to embrace the ups and the downs of life with joyful hearts and build lifelong bonds with our families.

### 3. Nourishing Identity

Shaping our children's minds and hearts builds character, grit, and endurance, but we can take it a step further. Abundant life is more readily available when a child fully embraces their God-given identity. The third growth area to purposefully nourish in our children is their identity.

When it comes to identity, we'll thoroughly inspect how we view ourselves. I've seen too many parents miss the fullness of God's promises because they don't understand their spiritual identity and what it means to be a child of the Most High God. When we don't look to God, we start looking to other people and the world to tell us who we are.

Sometimes those well-meaning voices conflict with what God speaks over our lives and we start to feel less than. As if we need to earn God's acceptance and love. The problem is, we're already loved more than we could ever imagine by the God who spoke every star into existence. And right now, He is speaking a better word over you.

When parents discover the rights they have as God's children, they're better equipped to shape their children's identities. By knowing who you were created to be, you find your true purpose. Wouldn't it be awesome if our children could walk with confidence early on, knowing they're exactly where God wants them to be?

As we saw in the mind section, intentionally developing this when a child is young produces a harvest later in life. According to research by George Barna, a person develops most of their moral foundations by the age of nine.[5] Furthermore, "In essence, what you believe by the time you are 13 is what you will die believing."[6] Children are impressionable and have the ability to form lasting beliefs when they are little. While reading a devotional and praying with our kids before bed is good, we can do more to shape a child's moral foundation. In these chapters, we'll learn strategies to help our kids genuinely *experience* the goodness of God at a young age. So, when they're old, they won't depart from it.

Along with learning about spiritual development, we'll discover how to intentionally build a child's self-esteem. The early years lay the foundation for not only cognitive and spiritual development but also self-worth. By the age of five, children develop a sense of self-esteem comparable in strength to that of an adult.[7] Before they enter kindergarten, young children already have a positive or negative sense of self.

If your kids are older, I don't want this statistic to discourage you. There is no question that neural connections form most quickly in the early years, but new connections continue to develop throughout one's life span.[8] There's still hope! It may take more effort and perseverance to change already established brain patterns, but change *is* possible. It's never too late to build healthy neural connections.

That being said, if we know self-esteem develops early and is relatively stable through one's life span, why not capitalize on this developmental leap early? Instead of sitting back and hoping our kids feel good about themselves, we can intentionally build positive God-centered identities and self-esteem in our children today. We can use specific parenting strategies to nurture a child's self-worth and raise kids who have grit, perseverance, and compassion.

Waiting until our kids are teenagers to look at what shapes their minds, hearts, and identities is a mistake. The Center on the Developing Child at Harvard University states, "It is easier and less costly to form strong brain circuits during the early years than it is to intervene or 'fix' them later."[9] We need to purposefully lay the groundwork in our children's formative years of development. The foundation built in the first five years of life will impact future growth for years to come.

## Walking It Out at Home

After we learn the specific strategies to parent with purpose, we'll bring it all together in the home section. This is where we discover how to live out these principles for a lifetime. We've made some big changes, and now we need to learn how to walk them out on a day-to-day basis.

First, we'll look at the atmosphere of our homes. Regardless of how much we emphasize spiritual and emotional health, if our homes are chaotic, growth won't take place at the rate we desire. We want to make our homes a place of refuge where kids can grow well.

We end the home section by looking at our daily rhythms. Our daily routines and rhythms dictate our destinies. We'll ask ourselves the following questions: What is the focus of our home? What are our children learning, intentionally or unintentionally, in our home? And how can we schedule true rest for our families? Through these chapters, we'll discover the difference between soul care and self-care and why we need both. We'll end by making a plan to daily live out these godly principles with our families.

Being intentional about creating a home filled with grace, love, patience, and discipline reminds me of the children's song about the wise man building his house upon the rock. As a child, I always wondered exactly what that meant and how I'd know whether my house was built on sand or rock.

But now as an adult, I have a clearer picture of Jesus's warning in Matthew 7:24–25. I love how The Passion Translation puts it:

> Everyone who hears my teaching and applies it to his life can be compared to a wise man who built his house on an unshakable foundation. When the rains fell and the flood came, with fierce winds beating upon his house, it stood firm because of its strong foundation.

No one is exempt from the storms of life. The rain will surely come, but the ground on which we build our houses has a great deal to do with how we weather the storm. Are we purposefully laying the foundation in our children's lives? Are we diligently pursuing Jesus's heart and teachings each day as a family? When we intentionally build godly homes, our family's firm foundation cannot be shaken.

## Perfection Isn't Required

Now, I want you to take a deep breath. If you're anything like me, when you read statistics and information about how to raise strong, healthy kids, you immediately panic and worry about what you've done wrong so far as a parent. Or you start spiraling, thinking about how you'll never be able to live up to the impossible standard you set for yourself. You can find something positive in all of this. Parents who practice purposeful parenting when their children are young reap great rewards later in life. Note that I didn't say *perfect* parenting. I said *purposeful* parenting.

We may not always get it exactly right; we will make mistakes. In my earlier story about taking my toddler for a walk, I stayed calm and peacefully addressed her. But trust me, there have been many times when I didn't remain calm, cool, and collected. I've lost my temper with my kids.

The enemy wants us to believe that when we mess up, there's no moving forward. That's simply not the case. Even in those messy moments, we can show our children the value of confessing sin, asking for forgiveness, and offering an apology. Kids need to know their parents make mistakes, just like them. We can guide them in how to right their wrongs. God forgives us freely of our sins, and we need to offer ourselves the same forgiveness when we make mistakes in our parenting journeys.

At the end of the day, we do the best we can and give the rest to God. Then we make a conscious decision to refuse the lies of the enemy that we don't have any hope of raising strong, good kids. With God's help, we can intentionally train our children to be strong in the Lord.

If you walk away with anything from this chapter, I pray it's this: our kids need firm foundations, and God commissioned us as their parents to cultivate them. We can't do it alone, but we have a great partner who walks alongside us. With God's help, we can take hold of these formative years and see the blessing of instilling value and identity into their hearts and minds.

# PART 1

# Nurturing Your Child's Mind, Heart, and Identity

# 3

# Your Thoughts Have Power

I'm sure you've heard the saying "Opposites attract." The expression is very true in my marriage and something I'm grateful for almost every day. There's a reason my dad and brother nicknamed me "Miss Melodramatic Lauren" as a child. I feel things deeply, and in less than sixty seconds, I can move from being cool, calm, and collected to frazzled and flustered. Thankfully, one of the most accurate words to describe my husband is steady. He's exceptionally even-keeled, bringing a beautiful balance to our marriage.

Last winter, I could've used his laid-back composure when dealing with our sick child. This child seems to share my knack for being sensitive. Her nose became so stuffy from a head cold that she wasn't able to breathe. When she tried to lie down to sleep, she needed to breathe through her mouth. She did *not* like that feeling. Shortly after being tucked in, she came to our bedroom telling me she couldn't sleep. I watched as panic slowly swept across her face. I recognized her expression. It felt familiar because I'd given it to my husband many times before.

Tears formed in her eyes as she voiced her distress. I'd already given her cough medicine, put eucalyptus salve on her chest, and sprayed her nose with saline. I couldn't think of anything else to do to help her feel better physically.

I gave her a big hug and told her, "You'll be fine. Just try to relax. Think good thoughts. I want you to say out loud, 'It's going to be okay.'" She listened and said what I'd asked, but I could tell it wasn't helping. Her feelings about the situation did not change no matter how hard I tried to cheer her up.

*Quick, Lauren, think.* Finally, my school psychology training came back to me. There was one thing left to try. I had to address her mind. The negative thought loop in her brain had caused panic and tears, which only made her nose stuffier. Her fears had also activated her sympathetic nervous system, or fight-or-flight response. When our nervous systems are on high alert, adrenaline starts to course through our bloodstream. I needed to stop her downward thought spiral and get her out of fight-or-flight mode to turn the situation around.

But how? In the moment, she couldn't see that her thoughts had anything to do with her distress.

How do we handle situations where our children don't recognize that their thoughts are causing them more discomfort than the actual situation? It's tough because mindsets take time to change, but there's a simple strategy that can bring peace to the brain quickly.

## Calming an Anxious Mind

Cognitive distractions are powerful when we're trying to stop a downward thought spiral. For adults, a cognitive distraction could look like challenging a negative thought with a truth-filled statement or meditating on a peaceful thought. We disrupt the negative thought loop right away by adding in new information, stopping it from progressing. Unfortunately, many of us don't use this technique; instead, we try to suppress the negative thought. However, that tends to only intensify the worry.

Some children may be able to use positive statements or Scripture to challenge their thinking, but other kids may benefit from using simple activities to redirect and distract their minds from the worry. In the moment, it's helpful to have a strategy that works.

Though I must warn you that this is a temporary solution. If we continue to suppress those unhelpful thoughts without getting to the root of the problem, the loops will continue to show up. In chapter 4, we'll learn how to get to the bottom of the unhelpful thoughts so we won't have to keep distracting our brains.

Knowing my daughter's personality and how much she loves to read, I grabbed a book and took her into the bathroom with me. I turned on a hot shower for steam and asked her to start reading out loud. Within seconds of reading, I saw peace wash

**Brain Builder:** Here is your first brain builder activity! While reading can be a useful cognitive distraction for adults and children, grounding exercises can also soothe an anxious mind. If you or your child can't seem to escape an unhelpful thought loop, try one of these activities. At first glance, the exercises seem simple, almost too simple, but they really work to calm an overstimulated mind.

1. Name all the fruits and vegetables you can think of that start with the letter A. Then work your way through the alphabet.
2. Find something in the room that starts with the letter A . . . B . . . C . . . and keep searching until you make it to Z.
3. Look around the room and find red-colored objects, then find things with orange. Work your way through the rainbow.

Try one of these exercises the next time you or your child feels overstimulated. Through trial and error, you'll find which one works best for you and your family.

over her face. She had to concentrate on reading the words. Reading aloud created a cognitive distraction, stopping her negative thought spiral. She couldn't use her brainpower to both read and worry. After a few minutes of the steamy shower and a good book, she went happily to bed and slept soundly through the night. The distractions successfully stopped the negative thought spiral and helped her downregulate her nervous system.

That evening I learned a powerful lesson. When a child is distraught, our first instinct is to soothe their emotions or correct their misbehavior, when instead we should address their mind. My daughter experienced a mental block, and she needed help lifting it. Thankfully, I found an effective way to bring peace to her mind.

The first time our children experience anxious thoughts can feel overwhelming as a parent. We may worry that if we don't respond in the best way, we'll somehow further damage them. But instead of living in fear, we can equip ourselves with the right tools to help our children stop negative thought spirals and find mental clarity. As we walk through the mind section, we may even find some of these tools helpful for transforming our own thoughts. Remember, emotionally healthy parents raise emotionally healthy kids. As we grow in our ability to pay attention to our thoughts, we'll be better equipped to shape our children's brains for good.

## Transform Your Life by Taking Control of Your Thoughts

At some point, all of us *will* face stressful, uncomfortable, and challenging situations. No matter how hard we try, we can't avoid adversity.

Whenever life gets tough, it's natural to look for a reason for our trouble. This is especially true for kids, whose first instinct may be to blame people, places, or things for their distress. My kids often say things like "I'm so bored. I want to go somewhere, then I'll have fun" or "Her singing is so annoying. I can't handle her. She's making me so mad." The funny thing is that complaining about a sibling's behavior only seems to increase that aggravating behavior. Why do siblings love to purposefully irritate each other? Whatever the reason, when we feel cranky, we tend to focus on all the things going wrong and mistakenly tell ourselves, *If only my situation changed, then I'd be happy, peaceful, calm,* _____. The problem with that thinking is we can't control everything that happens to us.

The good news is we *can* control how we respond to adversity. I often tell my kids, "The only person who has control over your happiness is you." We tend to limit ourselves from experiencing joy, peace, and contentment because we waste time blaming our problems on everything around us. Our circumstances don't need to change to bring us peace. It's our thoughts that need transformation.

If you want to change your life, change your thoughts.

## Understanding How Our Thoughts Impact Our Lives

Kids who are confident, filled with self-control, and have a well-balanced mind know how their thoughts influence their everyday life. To intentionally build strong mental pathways in our children, we need to see how everything interconnects. When I worked as a school psychologist, my students knew about the cognitive triangle. It's one of the best tools I've found to teach children (and adults) how their thoughts influence their emotions and everyday life. To keep things simple, we'll draw on my daughter's stuffy nose story to demonstrate how to utilize the cognitive triangle with your kids. You can follow these same steps and use the diagram below with any difficult situation you walk through as well.

While I'm known to grab a piece of paper and draw out a cognitive triangle at the kitchen table, I've found it's best to discuss how thoughts and feelings interconnect after a stressful situation. In the middle of the struggle, we often don't have the perspective or mental energy to think clearly. Also, note that the first few times you use the cognitive triangle with your kids, they may need some help correctly reflecting on and identifying their feelings, thoughts, and behaviors. Before you offer your insight, give them a few minutes to ponder and assess.

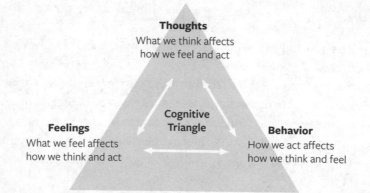

**Thoughts**
What we think affects
how we feel and act

**Cognitive
Triangle**

**Feelings**
What we feel affects
how we think and act

**Behavior**
How we act affects
how we think and feel

Let's look at feelings first. Typically, this triangle point is one of the simpler sides to work through, but it still may take some digging. Kids as young as two years old can use basic terms such as happiness, sadness, anger, and fear to talk about their emotions.[1] While that's true, some children may need more vocabulary or insight to correctly identify how they feel about certain situations or events. It takes time for them to be able to recognize what anger feels like in their body, and it takes practice to express it in words.

I've seen many children who were clearly nervous or anxious about a situation but had no idea how to read the signals their bodies sent them. Kids may not recognize that the fluttery feeling they get in their chest means they feel nervous or that tightness in their jaw means they feel mad. They may not know what those physical sensations signify the first few times they feel them.

48

I remember an eight-year-old girl telling me before a big race, "I don't know what's happening. I'm excited, but I also feel jittery." She felt anxious, but she didn't know it. When I told her she could feel excited and nervous simultaneously, she was shocked. She said, "I never knew you could feel both emotions at the same time! I've never felt this way before."

Many kids and adults may be able to quickly identify the first emotion they feel in a situation, but don't rush this step. Take time to dig deeper and sit in that feeling. Are any other emotions present? Before moving on too quickly, ask your child to

## 🔒 Helping Your Child Understand and Identify Their Feelings

Some children can express their feelings very quickly starting at a young age. Other children may need more guidance or instruction about how to correctly identify what they feel and how to describe it. Here are two strategies to help your child better understand emotion.

*Feelings Chart*. Charts that detail the different emotions and show physical cues of what feelings look like can be beneficial for children. Use the chart to talk about what anger or boredom feels like and looks like in their body. Discuss times when they may have felt the different emotions.

*Draw it Out*. We often want our children to tell us exactly what they feel using words, but that can be difficult when they're in the middle of a big feeling. Instead of nagging the child to tell you, grab a piece of paper and ask the child to draw out their feelings. Say something like "What do your feelings look like right now? What does it feel like in your body? Draw it here to show me." If your child is old enough, they can journal instead of drawing or talking it out.

A child's ability to read emotions is invaluable. Once kids learn to identify exactly what they are feeling, they can start to regulate their emotions.

describe what their body feels like when they experience the specific emotion they identified.

After your child identifies the feelings, move to the behavior. If they exhibited negative behavior such as hitting or yelling, they may struggle to correctly identify this point of the triangle.

As a school psychologist and parent, I've heard a lot of "yeah, but she hit me first" or "he made me do it." Kids will try to justify their misbehavior or blame it on someone or something else. If you experience the blame game with your kids, gently remind them that the focus of the activity isn't to label other people's behaviors. Tell them they're going to focus on their actions because they're responsible for their behavior. We can't control what other people do or say. Then bring your child back to labeling all their actions in the given situation.

My daughter's actions included pacing the room and crying. In this example, can you see how feeling anxious prompted her to walk around nervously? As you fill in the triangle, begin to draw connections between the points. What connections can you and your child make about their specific situation?

Finally, consider their thoughts. Life is busy and their attention and focus are often divided. This causes many kids to miss the thoughts running through their minds. To fully understand the situation, we must help them intentionally slow down and think about what their brain is telling them. Ask your child, "What were you thinking in the situation?" Write down everything they say. Then ask, "Were your thoughts helpful or unhelpful?"

In the stuffy nose scenario, my daughter thought, *I'll never be able to fall asleep. I hate how this feels.* Can you see how those thoughts brought her angst instead of peace? Her thoughts influenced her feelings, which influenced her actions.

The idea that we have thoughts running through our minds at all times may be new and surprising to your child. You might find it a bit surprising, too, if you've never thought about your thoughts before. Maybe you've heard people say, "You must take every thought captive," but you have no idea how to actually do that. By the end of this chapter, you'll learn exactly how to identify your mental meditations and discover how to teach your kids to do the same. When you do this, you'll begin to see how your thoughts influence your everyday actions.

Whenever your child experiences a hard situation, make sure they process all three aspects of the triangle at the same time. How did their thoughts influence their emotions? Their behavior? Consider how all of it interconnects. Then ask your child which point of the triangle will be the easiest to change. Hint: it's not their behavior.

Remember when I told my daughter to just calm down? It didn't work. If only we could change our feelings by snapping our fingers. Additionally, telling a child to simply stop being anxious or quit having tantrums won't fix the problem. Changing our feelings and actions can be difficult, but know this: breakthrough is possible regardless of whether the people or circumstances surrounding us change.

We find change by paying attention to our thoughts. We can't ignore what our mind tells us.

## What Does Science Say about the Power of Our Thoughts?

You may be thinking, *Okay, I've heard many people say thoughts matter, but how much could they possibly impact my life or my child's life? Our thoughts are generally good. They can't be that powerful.*

Researchers continue to discover how greatly our minds impact our behavior, health, and happiness. Andrew Newberg, a neuroscientist at Thomas Jefferson University, and Mark Robert Waldman, an expert in communication, studied how our thoughts influence our everyday lives. They found that when we focus on negative words and thoughts, we disrupt not only our sleep and our appetites but also the pathways our brains use to regulate happiness, longevity, and health.[2] Our thoughts hold so much power, they even shape the structure of our brains. Something we can't physically see causes physical reshaping.

We need to start paying attention to the words we think and speak because they make a lasting difference. Even in children. Researchers found negative self-talk in children plays a role in their anxiety levels.[3] Our thoughts influence the quality of our lives. Whether or not we realize it, our internal dialogue affects our health and happiness.

If unhelpful thoughts cause disruption, helpful thoughts should bring healing. Research suggests thinking positively provides health benefits such as increased life span, better psychological and physical well-being, and even greater resistance to the common cold.[4] Not only that, Newberg and Waldman remark in *Words Can Change Your Brain,*

> Our own brain-scan research shows that concentrating and meditating on positive thoughts, feelings, and outcomes can be more powerful than any drug in the world, especially when it comes to changing old habits, behaviors, and beliefs. And to the best of our knowledge, the entire process is driven by the language-based processes of the brain.[5]

*More powerful than any drug in the world.* Let that sink in for a second. Our thoughts and language bring us either joy or dread. Life or death. Emotionally healthy kids and adults know the power of the mind and learn how to harness its power. God was right when He said the power of life and death is in the tongue (Prov. 18:21).

A quick sidenote on positive thinking. Thinking positively doesn't mean we should ignore tough situations or negative emotions. That's called toxic positivity and not something I recommend. Denying reality can be harmful because our negative feelings won't magically disappear if we pretend they don't exist. That's not what I'm talking about here. We need to find a healthy balance of positivity. So instead of always thinking about the worst-case scenario, we choose to believe God is good and His foundation for us is love.

## What Does the Bible Say about the Power of Our Thoughts?

I love it when research complements the truth of Scripture. Science is finally catching up to what God wrote thousands of years ago.

> Pleasant words are like a honeycomb,
> Sweetness to the soul and health to the bones. (Prov. 16:24)

> For as he thinks in his heart so is he. (Prov. 23:7)

Our words directly affect our health. Our thoughts dictate who we become. I believe God knew the true power of our thoughts, because why else would He tell us to hold every thought captive (2 Cor. 10:5)? The mind is where everything starts. Seeds of doubt, lies, and fear are first established in the mind. Then they exalt themselves against the knowledge of God.

Oftentimes when we feel stuck or need a change in our life, a stronghold (lie, doubt, or fear) first needs to be removed. A stronghold is a fortress or tower that cannot be penetrated. We may not be able to remove mental towers with our own strength, but thankfully, God tells us that when we use His mighty weapons, we can remove strongholds and align our minds with Christ.

Taking every thought captive and transforming our thoughts isn't easy. However, I've seen tremendous breakthroughs in children (and adults) when they take thought inventories and intentionally nurture their minds. As we learn how the mind works, we can build a strong foundation in our children's brains. If we want to raise emotionally healthy children, they must understand the power of their thoughts and how their mind influences their everyday lives.

## The First Step to Building a Powerful Mind: Practicing Metacognition

One of the first steps to building a healthy mind is practicing metacognition, or the act of thinking about what you're thinking about. You can't conquer something that you know nothing about. Before you pull down strongholds, you must become aware of your brain's thought patterns and neural pathways. You can't control what you don't recognize. Doing this takes practice. With over seventy thousand thoughts per day, you can see why this skill takes time to master.[6] Soon you'll learn how to explain metacognition to your child using kid-friendly terminology. But first, I want you to practice the skill yourself.

**Brain Builder:** Let's pause for a moment and practice metacognition. Set your timer for three minutes and take an inventory of your thoughts. Grab a piece of paper and intentionally write down every thought that comes to your mind. It doesn't matter what the thought is. If you think it, write it down.

Did you take a thought inventory? During this time, you may have noticed your mind wandered a bit. You may have even thought about two completely different things simultaneously. Can you see how it could be easy for a negative thought to slip through your consciousness and go undetected? Though your brain doesn't actively engage with every thought, even the fleeting ones impact your mood and behavior. With practice, you can begin to recognize your thoughts and bind the unhelpful ones before they become too entrenched in your brain. By harnessing the negative thoughts, you will learn to hold every thought captive. Even young children can practice metacognition.

Hey, before you sit down and try the Brain Builder on the next page, I want you to hear this: The activity may not go exactly as planned. Actually, I can almost guarantee the conversation won't go as scripted. If that's the case, you haven't done anything wrong. Your family is totally normal. Building your child's spiritual and emotional health is more than one five-minute conversation. These activities are meant to be used as a guide and things you can bring into your everyday life over time. It's okay if your real-life conversation looks different from the one here.

As the parent, you decide if you want your children to tell you their thoughts after the three minutes or if you want them to write down their thoughts as time elapses. The goal of the exercise is to help your child become aware of their thoughts. Intentional pauses help them listen to their mind. If they moan and complain about completing the activity, don't let that stop you from trying. That being said, if you face massive amounts of resistance, maybe try it for only one minute instead of three or stop the activity completely and try it again another day. With time and repetition, you and your children can get good at knowing your thoughts and making sure the things you think bring you life, not dread.

The art of metacognition and the skill of identifying our hidden thoughts take time and practice. They won't happen overnight. But with repetition, rehearsal, and perseverance, we can intentionally rewire our brains to think more positive or helpful thoughts. Each morning we have the opportunity to shape our minds.

Dr. Caroline Leaf, a leading neuroscientist and mind expert, beautifully explains the process like this:

> Every morning when you wake up, new baby nerve cells have been born while you were sleeping that are there at your disposal

**Brain Builder:** Take five minutes today to practice metacognition with your children. Start by explaining the power of your words.

Say something like "How did God create the world? Did He do it with His hands? Tools?" Pause for a moment and let your child answer.

Then say, "He did it by speaking a word. In Genesis 1:3, we read 'And God said, "Let there be light," and there was light (NIV).' That's it. God created our world with His words. Isn't that amazing? That's why we often tell you to speak kindly to others. Our words matter.

"Here's another fascinating fact. Did you know the universe is continually expanding? It's been growing ever since God spoke it into existence. Every minute space is stretching, and it's all because of the words God spoke in the beginning. Words carry power. But before we ever speak a word, it starts as a thought in our mind.

"Today we're going to practice thinking about what we're thinking about so we can make sure our words bring life to our lives. We think thousands of thoughts every day. We may not always be aware of what our thoughts tell us, but we can learn to listen to our minds. It's important to practice this skill because our thoughts and words make a lasting difference. Right now, let's take three minutes away from all distractions (no electronics, music, toys, snacks, etc.) to think about what we are thinking about."

to be used in tearing down toxic thoughts and rebuilding healthy thoughts. The birth of these new baby nerve cells is called neurogenesis, which brings to mind "The LORD's mercies . . . are new every morning" (Lam. 3:23).[7]

Each day provides us with another opportunity to take charge of our thoughts and build healthier, more productive thought loops.

## The Second Step to Building a Powerful Mind: Learning to Reflect

Before we learn to uproot those deeply hidden unconscious thoughts, there's one more practical tool we can use to help us understand our mental patterns. Dr. Albert Ellis, a world-renowned psychotherapist, developed the ABC method to help people understand the connection between their perspective or mental framework and their behaviors and beliefs.

When we break down a situation and reflect on our actions and beliefs, we gain valuable insight into the lens or framework through which we view the world. Too often, we don't immediately see our distorted lens. Instead, we think if our situation changed, then we could be happy. We don't see that our thoughts and beliefs, not our circumstances, prevent us from living a full life. Think of how much heartache and frustration could be spared if a child learned how to analyze these frameworks and connections accurately at a young age.

Let's learn how to use the ABC method to reflect on a past event or present problem. A stands for adversity or the situation we find ourselves in. B stands for beliefs or what we tell ourselves about the situation. Finally, C stands for consequences or the actions we take because of the beliefs we hold. Using this model, we can create a thought journal. As we inspect what happened before, during, and after the event and exactly what we were feeling, we will find thought patterns we tend to use.

Let me give you an example of a thought pattern I often got stuck in early in motherhood. A: Today my kids are being extra whiny, constantly asking me for a snack, and arguing with each other over every little thing. B: My life is so hard. My kids are so annoying. I just need a break. C: I'm angry and upset. I yell at my children and blame them for my distress.

In the next exercise, we'll dig deeper into our thought lives to see if our thoughts help or discourage us. Both children and

**Brain Builder:** Complete the thought log on the next page and take the time to fully assess the situation. After you complete it, go back to the belief section. Ask yourself or your child the following questions to determine if your beliefs were helpful, accurate, and true:
- Is the belief true? Provide evidence.
- Is your perspective or belief completely accurate?
- Is the belief helpful?
- If your beliefs changed, would it result in a different consequence?

adults can use the ABC thought log to gain insight into their mental patterns.

Sometimes our beliefs may be true and accurate. Life with small kids at home *is* hard, especially when we don't have a lot of support from family or friends. Our belief that we feel stuck and like we need a break is based on truth. That's when we push further and ask, How is this belief influencing my thoughts? When I focus on this truth, does it improve the situation or keep me discouraged? At times both adults and kids will find themselves in tough situations. Especially during those times, we need to step back and assess our overall perspective.

If I constantly meditate on how hard my life is, I'll continue to feel discouraged. However, if I recognize, yes, this is hard, but harping on the negative is not helping me, I can shift my beliefs from "this is too hard" to "this is hard, but I can still find good moments in my day, and I choose to focus on those instead." I can change my beliefs or thoughts. And as a result, my reactions to a hard day will change too.

Use this concrete thought log for yourself or your children as often as needed. As you start to reflect more on your beliefs and thoughts, you may notice certain patterns.

## ABC THOUGHT LOG

**A**dversity: Use your five senses to describe the situation. What happened right before and during the event?

**B**eliefs: What went through your head at the time? What were you telling yourself about the event? What did you believe about the situation?

**C**onsequences: How did the adversity make you feel? How did you respond to the situation? Write down your reactions, behaviors, and feelings in this section.

In the next chapter, we'll look at the most common mental mistakes kids and adults make. Then we'll learn how to challenge that wrong thinking and take control of our thoughts before they start to control us.

For our kids to become mentally strong, they must learn to pay attention to their thoughts. As parents, we can help our children learn to accurately assess their thoughts. A healthy mind knows what's running through it. With intentional mindfulness, kids can spot those negative thought loops before they progress too far. Our brains can work for us instead of against us.

# 4

# Overcoming the Most Common Mental Mistakes

I used to think if I thought positive thoughts for one day, I'd be emotionally healthy. But removing negative mindsets and replacing them with life-giving thoughts takes time, discipline, and perseverance. I like to think of the process like exfoliating your face; instead of skin renewal, it's mind renewal. The first step is always to wash, clean, and remove any dead skin by identifying dead thoughts and scrubbing them off. We started the removal process in chapter 3 by learning to pay attention to our thoughts.

Now we need to scrub a little deeper to completely eliminate those unhelpful mindsets. In this chapter, you'll learn about the seven common mental mistakes people make that hold them back from complete mental freedom. As you learn about the following frameworks, you'll find Brain Builders under each mindset to help you reframe, refocus, and renew your mind.

Finally, after the skin is scrubbed and exposed, we'll add in some deep moisture by learning to fix our thoughts on heavenly things and letting go of everything else. The last step brings everything together and keeps your mind anchored in truth.

Meditating on lovely and excellent things is a great practice, and you may want to move straight to the moisturizer because of the comfort it provides. But if you genuinely want to rewire your brain and bring complete wholeness to your thought life, you can't skip the first two steps. Exposing negative mindsets is hard work. Nevertheless, it's essential to take the time to exfoliate. If we add in the moisturizer before removing all the dead skin, we won't experience complete restoration. Let's not move too quickly through this process or we may miss some deeply rooted lies taking hold in our minds.

## Inviting the Holy Spirit In

The first step in identifying our most common thinking mistakes is to invite the Holy Spirit into the process. Sometimes our minds blind us from seeing the error in our thinking. With the Holy Spirit's help, we can push past the blindness and find the root of the issue. Let's ask the Holy Spirit to remove any clouds from our vision. He may even show us a different way to look at the situation.

*Heavenly Father, thank You for sending us the Holy Spirit, our helper, advocate, and comforter. Holy Spirit, right now I pray You open our spiritual eyes and ears to see things from Your perspective. We thank You that because You abide in us, we have Your anointing. Holy Spirit, may Your anointing teach us concerning all things. Illuminate any harmful mindsets we may be harboring or our children may be holding on to. Show us the truth, as only You can do. Pull down any strongholds that may be holding us or our children back from seeing God's glory and grace in our lives. In Jesus's mighty name we pray, amen.*

The Holy Spirit is essential in helping us transform our minds. We can't do it alone.

Now I need to warn you: all of us will experience distorted thinking at one point or another in our lives. It becomes a problem when skewed thinking turns into habitual practice. People with sound minds understand that thinking can become twisted, but that doesn't mean we have to stay stuck in those twisted thinking patterns. We can transform our thoughts and calm our minds with self-awareness and practical tools.

I also want you to understand that it's okay if you and your children make these mental mistakes. As a parent, I've found myself trapped in a few different toxic thinking mentalities over the years. I've even noticed my children starting to copy some of the same mental mistakes I make. Generations can pass on mindsets and strongholds. But the good news is, you're here today, ready to tackle those toxic thoughts. And the work you put in will help not only you but your children as well. Brain change is always possible.

## The "I'll Be Happy When . . ." Mentality

I still remember the day my then-future husband asked me why I wanted children. I responded with such joy and expectation, "Because it's going to be fun!" After the birth of our first child, I quickly found the job of raising children became a busy to-do list with little to no time for fun. Soon I felt exhausted and worn down by the mental, emotional, and spiritual demands of parenthood. I told myself I'd be happy one day in the future.

*I'll be happy when my daughter sleeps through the night.*
*I'll be happy when my kids can make their own breakfast.*
*I'll be happy when I won't be needed so much.*

The trouble was, my happiness kept getting delayed. As my mind repeated these lies—that happiness comes only when XYZ happens—my heart began to accept a false narrative. I fell into the trap of believing my happiness depended on my circumstances. I've seen children make this same mental mistake.

*I'll be happy when it's summer and I don't have to go to school.*

*I'll be happy when my brother stops bugging me.*

*I'll be happy when I make the soccer team.*

These lies create cycles of negative thoughts in our minds and dissatisfaction in our hearts, leading to destructive reactions and responses. That's no way to live.

As you start to identify some of the lies your heart believes and your mind repeats, think of rebuttals of truth you can use to combat them. Whenever I'm in a funk and think I'll never be happy again, I practice gratitude. It sounds simple, but it works. It shifts my perspective from "happiness is a far-off goal" to "goodness is around me, right here, right now."

Sharing one thing you're thankful for will help your family get into the habit of practicing gratitude and savoring the good. Research shows that the act of savoring or slowing down and enjoying the moment boosts overall levels of happiness and well-being.

**Brain Builder:** At dinner tonight, go around the kitchen table and take turns sharing at least one thing you felt thankful for today.

What does savoring look like in everyday life? University of Pennsylvania psychologist Martin Seligman suggests taking time once a day to slow down and enjoy something you usually hurry through—for example, eating a meal, taking a shower, or walking to class.[1] How did you feel when you slowed down compared to when you rushed through it? We're always in a hurry to get to the next best thing, but we can overcome the "I'll be happy when . . ." mentality by learning to live in the moment and make the most of everyday life. Don't give your circumstances or your hopes and dreams for the future permission to steal the joy available to you today.

## The Dramatic Mentality

When we feel upset or hurt, we tend to use words like *always* or *never* in speech and thought. Adults may think:

> I **never** do it well enough; she **always** finds something wrong with my work. My husband **always** gets to do what he wants, and I **never** get to do what I want to do.

Kids may think:

> She **always** gets to go first, and it's not fair! He **always** gets to pick what we watch. I **never** get a turn. She **never** has to sit in time-out, and I **always** have to.

Kids and adults get caught in this mindset from time to time. The problem with this thinking is that it exaggerates the truth. When we take the time to ponder the situation, it's most likely not as extreme as we perceive it to be. Our spouses, siblings, or friends don't *always* get to do what they want. Maybe that's true more often than we'd like, but it's unlikely that it's always accurate. If you or your child get stuck in this type of thinking, it's helpful to step back and look at the situation from a new perspective. The following Brain Builder will help you get a fresh outlook.

Checking your children's thoughts helps them see that sometimes they aren't helpful. My son and I were talking about this phenomenon in the car the other day, and he said, "But why are our thoughts against us?" It's true our brains can get into a habit of thinking unhelpful thoughts, but I made sure to explain to my son that this is why we take thought inventories. Then our thoughts can work for us instead of against us.

With practice, it gets easier to find unhelpful thought patterns that frustrate or aggravate us. The ability to reframe the situation into something more positive gets easier with practice too. We may not always have control over the first thought that comes to our mind, but as we become more aware of our thoughts, we can intentionally choose the ones that follow.

**Brain Builder:** The next time you or your child says a phrase with the word *always* or *never* in it, pause for a moment and then write it down. You should also record any other thoughts that come to mind related to your initial one.

After your list is complete, highlight the unhelpful thoughts. Then ask yourself, *Is the thought true?* As you brainstorm, think of how you can reframe the initial statement so that it's more helpful.

A phrase frequently heard in my house is "I'm bored." I don't make a big to-do every time I hear it, but if I notice my kids are stuck in this thought and unable to move forward, I may have a conversation that looks something like the following.

Unhelpful Thought: I'm *always* bored at home.

*Pause and Make a List with Your Child.* I may say something like "Tell me more about that" to get my child talking. She responds, "I have nothing to do. I'm so bored. It's always boring at home." I grab a piece of paper and write down all the child's thoughts and complaints. Then I ask my child, "Which statement on this list is true? Which statement makes you feel better? When was the last time you felt happy at home? Can you tell me about it?"

*Reframe.* My child may respond with, "Yes, it's true. Our house is always so boring. I don't know if these thoughts help me or not. Last week, when I built a fort with my brother, we had fun." To continue the conversation, I add, "Yes, you had a great time. You didn't want to stop playing to eat dinner. Sometimes being at home can be boring, but you've found ways to have fun in the past. Can we brainstorm together a few enjoyable activities that you can do right now?"

## Jumping to Conclusions

A third common type of wrong thinking is jumping to conclusions. We make a snap judgment based on a little bit of information and soon find ourselves in a negative thought spiral. This mental mistake can add endless worry and stress to our lives. We may see or hear something that initially upsets our spirit and right away jump to the worst-case scenario. We make assumptions based on how we initially feel about a situation. The trouble is, sometimes our interpretations are wrong because we haven't gathered all the facts.

Relationships seem to be an area where the jumping to conclusions mentality happens often. A few years ago, I saw a picture pop up on Facebook with my friends out to eat at a local restaurant. Immediately, my heart skipped a beat as I thought, *Why didn't they invite me? Too* quickly my thoughts spiraled to *I don't have any friends. Why is making friends so hard? Why don't they like me?* However, when I talked to my friends later, I found out the get-together was last minute, and they didn't intentionally exclude me. I shouldn't have followed my gut reaction.

Kids can make this same mental mistake. My elementary-aged kids have come home from school saying, "She doesn't like me" or "He doesn't ever want to play with me," but when I ask them how they know that, they can't provide any evidence. Before we jump to conclusions, we need to gather all the facts.

**Brain Builder:** If you notice yourself or your child affected by unnecessary worry, stop and write down everything about the situation. Then ask yourself or your child if there could be a different explanation for the situation. Take some deep breaths and try to gather more information before you let anxious thoughts take over.

If you can't get the information right away and need a quick solution, try a cognitive distraction like we discussed in chapter 3. Another idea is to talk to a trusted friend. When you share the situation, they may have a different perspective and be able to pray with you to help you calm your mind.

When we jump to conclusions, we waste countless hours worrying about something that may not even be true. Before we judge prematurely, we need to search out the facts.

## Focusing on the Bad

Another common mental mistake we make is ignoring the positive and focusing on the bad. Even when something good comes along, we dismiss it because it doesn't fit our negative mental framework. This type of thinking causes us to believe the lie that everything in our life is negative.

Have your children ever been frustrated with a task they couldn't figure out? In their frustration, they may have thought to themselves, *I can't do anything right.* Then without warning, their mind started to look for evidence to confirm their initial negative bias. If they thought of a blessing or positive event, their mind pushed it away. Children and adults I know who make this mental mistake tend to believe things like the following:

*I've messed this up before; I'll probably mess it up this time too.*

*That won't happen for me.*

*I bet this won't last long. Pretty soon something terrible will happen again.*

To break this cycle, we must accurately assess the situation, find the lie, then refute it with the truth. We most likely will need help from an outsider to do this successfully. Remember, our brains often try to push away conflicting evidence and confirm what we already believe.

Kids tend to get stuck in this negative mindset when they feel frustrated. They often see the world through their self-centered lens, which can make perspective-taking difficult for them. That's why talking with someone outside the situation can help children see the truth more clearly, forcing their minds out of the negative loop.

**Brain Builder:** To break free of the confirmation bias, it's helpful to talk through the situation with someone on the outside. Parents can help children find physical evidence to refute the lie and break the negative mindset. If you find your child stuck in this loop, brainstorm ways to show that the initial belief isn't true.

Here is an example: your child gets frustrated with his homework every night and says, "I can't do math. I'll never be able to do it." You could combat this thinking by writing down everything he can do or keeping track of all the times he has completed his math homework. Soon he'll see that there are many things he *can* do, and with perseverance (and maybe a little assistance), he *can* even do his math homework.

## Fear Mentality

God created us with a nervous system that activates to keep us safe. Our fight-or-flight response helps us discern when we need to avoid people, situations, or settings. This innate sense keeps us safe from danger. However, at times our response moves from healthy survival to unnecessary fear. In these cases, our fear is sometimes caused by a lack of trust in God.

Often when I fear, it's because I don't have faith that God is bigger than my situation. I so easily forget His promises, believing instead the false information around me, and lose sight of His faithfulness.

Fear is a sneaky thing because it's everywhere. During the height of the COVID-19 pandemic, my husband and I made sure our children didn't hear the news, and we tried not to talk about the virus in front of them. We didn't want to plant fear in their tiny hearts.

I'll never forget the look on my daughter's face when I told her my husband and I tested positive for COVID. She started crying

**Brain Builder:** Immediate ways to break free from the side effects of fear include breathing deeply, praying, practicing mindfulness by turning on a Christian meditation, exercising, stretching, going outside and smelling flowers, progressively relaxing our muscles, visualizing, or calling a friend.

In Cognitive Behavioral Therapy, this is called changing the channel. Essentially you take some kind of action to distract or reorient your brain.

A more long-term solution to break free from fear includes looking at what is feeding your family. What messages do you receive from screens, books, radio, the news, etc.? What is your spirit digesting daily? What are you doing to guard your heart and mind against anxious thoughts?

immediately. As she backed away from us, she said, "Okay, then I need to social distance from you. I have to stay six feet away." I had no idea how she knew to be so afraid. I asked her, "Where did you hear that you have to stay away from us?" She said, "I read it at swim class and the grocery store."

Duh, she can read! Her response to our sickness made me realize how important it is to have ongoing, open conversations with our children. We cannot protect them from every bit of negative information, but we can help them process it.

If you need help in this area, in chapter 5 we'll learn how to create an action plan to limit fear from entering our homes and spirits.

## Poor Me/Overgeneralization Mentality

Have you ever thought to yourself, *My life is so hard. Life is unfair. Are things going to stay this way forever?* When life gets hard, we can feel sorry for ourselves, and our flesh may be tempted to indulge those feelings of self-pity.

While adults do struggle with this mentality, children are more susceptible to it due to their lack of perspective. My children tend to struggle with it when they feel disappointed. For our family, it usually goes like this: I tell the kids we're going to a friend's house for dinner or for a family hike tomorrow, but then life happens and we end up canceling the plans because of some unforeseen circumstance. Due to the disappointment of unmet expectations, the kids struggle to bounce back.

When our children experience hardship or setbacks, providing comfort and a listening ear is tremendously beneficial. That's part of winning their hearts, but we need to be careful not to let them sit in the pain too long. God doesn't want us to stay stuck in our disappointment, frustration, or heartache. Many times, I've seen people take on a "woe is me" attitude when they were unable to move forward amid adversity.

Problems arise when kids use this framework for every situation in life. Soon they overgeneralize and think that if it happened before, it'll go the same way in the future. It could sound like "We never get to do anything fun. Our plans always get canceled and my life is terrible." Instead of hoping for the best, kids suppress the promise of God's goodness following them all the days of their lives.

Parents, in these circumstances we need Holy Spirit discernment. While it's valuable to sit with our children in their pain, we need to help them push through it. We don't want our children to become stuck in self-pity. In a state of self-indulgence, people tend to care only about themselves and miss seeing things from God's higher perspective.

When any of us deal with hardship, it's important to pay attention to our thoughts because it's in these moments that Satan whispers in our ears. "You're always going to be alone. You're never going to get to do anything fun. If God really loved you, why did He let this happen to you?" The enemy will do everything in his power to twist God's truth and make us doubt His great love for us. We need to bring these thoughts to Jesus's feet before a stronghold becomes implanted in our minds.

One of the best things parents can do is give their children permission to feel. The other day I had to cancel a playdate because I woke up feeling sick. Naturally my kids were sad. I gave them a big hug and said, "It's okay to feel sad." Sometimes we just need our feelings validated, then we can move forward. I followed up the validation with "What's something we can do instead to still have a good day?" Kids should be allowed to feel frustration, disappointment, or sadness, but the key is not staying stuck in the feeling.

**Brain Builder:** Some kinds of adversity are naturally more challenging than others, meaning in some cases our children will need more empathy and support from us than at other times. If a beloved pet passes away or a best friend moves to a different state, it's normal to feel upset. That's why we, as parents, need to pray and ask the Holy Spirit to instruct us on how to move forward when our children face life adversity. Different situations call for different responses. We need wisdom from God to find the best way to handle our children's emotions.

No matter the severity of the situation, resting on God's promises is always a good idea. I've found it helpful for myself and my children to meditate on a verse that speaks directly about the problem situation. Choose a promise in God's Word that brings light to the situation. If your children can write without assistance, have them write down the verse on a piece of paper and tape it next to their bathroom mirror. Then encourage them to say it out loud every morning when they see it.

## "I Should" Mentality

All of us make mistakes. No one gets it right all the time. We must learn to give ourselves grace in the process, because if we don't, we can become consumed with the thought *I should have* or *I wish I would have*. People say hindsight is 20/20. After the fact, we always seem to have a clearer picture of the situation and how we should have acted differently. While it's healthy to use the past as motivation to bring about a better future, difficulty arises when we get stuck in regret and beat ourselves up for our mistakes.

When we are discouraged and frustrated with ourselves every day, it's a sign that our perspective needs to shift. Years ago, I memorized Romans 3:23: "For all have sinned and fall short of the glory of God." It reminded me that none of us will ever be perfect. However, years later, I realized I missed out on everything God was trying to say by not memorizing verse 24 with it: "Being justified freely by His grace through the redemption that is in Christ Jesus." Yes, we were born sinners, but that isn't the end of the story. We have an opportunity to be in right standing with God, and He freely gives us this gift through grace. Why do we hold ourselves back from receiving it?

Although there are several other mindsets, these are the seven I see kids and adults use most often. As you worked through this chapter, you may have noticed that some of these Brain Builders seemed similar. Several of the activities have similar themes because there are only so many ways to fix wrong thinking. The goal of these activities is to get you and your child's mind to think in a new way.

Did you see yourself or your child in any of the mindsets? If you did, don't panic. Your brain is capable of change. You can remove old, dead ways of thinking and instead embrace the mind of Christ. It will take time. Be patient with yourself and your children. Certainly, God can do a creative miracle and instantly bring about the necessary change. But other times He may allow us to walk through the desert to get to the promised land. Take it one day at a time and keep fighting for your mind. Finding fresh perspectives comes with repetition. Rewiring your child's brain with right thinking takes time; it won't happen after one conversation. Keep practicing, and each day you do, your brain will slowly change.

Remember, we're exfoliating our minds, just like we do our faces. We want to get rid of the old stuff before locking in the good stuff. Before we move to the deep moisturizer, I want to give you three more tools to use as you mull over these mental mistakes. While the Brain Builders in this chapter should provide some relief to your mind, the following tools will bring that extra boost to help you eliminate old thought patterns and solidify new ones.

**Brain Builder:** Learn from your mistakes, but don't hold yourself in unnecessary mental bondage. J. Kim Penberthy, a professor of psychiatry and neurobehavioral sciences at the University of Virginia, recommends four steps to ease the grip of regret. "Rather than stay stuck, people can manage these emotions in four steps: First, accept the fact that you are feeling them; determine why you are feeling them; allow yourself to learn from them; and finally, release them and move forward."[2]

If you or your children find yourselves in this mentality often, take a few moments to write down your most frequent "I should" statements. Consider your thoughts. Where did they come from? What can you learn from them? Then pray alone or with your children and ask God to help you move forward. That means saying "I am forgiven" if you need to forgive yourself for not getting it right. Give yourself some of the grace that God freely gives to you. As far as the east is from the west, God forgives your transgressions (Ps. 103:12).

Take it a step further by considering the hope and future God has for you. If your children need help with this task, share with them examples of the gifts and talents you believe God has placed in their hearts. Dream of the future together and share ways you've seen God work in your own life.

## Write to Create New Pathways

First, if you want to rewire your brain or your child's brain and create new neural pathways, I highly recommend keeping a thought journal. Researchers have found that cursive handwriting helps the brain learn and remember better.[3] If you want to create new pathways in your brain, try writing down the new thought. The physical act of writing helps the brain encode the new information and store it in memory.[4]

It could be as simple as writing down a few Scripture verses you want to meditate on throughout the day or recording a new perspective to combat an old thought pattern. Your children can do this simple act to encourage positive thinking too. People say it takes twenty-one days to form a habit. If you or your children want to embrace a thought, take time to write it down in your journal every day for twenty-one days.

## Read Your Bible to Uncover Deep-Seated Beliefs

To uncover deep-seated negative beliefs, we need God's help. One of the best ways to unpack our innermost thoughts is by reading the Bible. Our motivation for reading God's Word shouldn't be that we want God to bless us or love us more. It also isn't something we should do because we want to be "good Christians." We read God's Word because it's alive, and it activates something within us when we read it.

> For the Word that God speaks is alive and full of power [making it active, operative, energizing, and effective]; it is sharper than any two-edged sword, penetrating to the dividing line of the breath of life (soul) and [the immortal] spirit, and of joints and marrow [of the deepest parts of our nature], exposing and sifting and analyzing and judging the very thoughts and purposes of the heart. (Heb. 4:12 AMPC)

The Word of God is full of power. Those hidden negative beliefs that we struggle to identify become completely exposed when we read and hear the Word. In our own strength, we may not be able to separate our heart's secret motives, but God's Word uncovers and separates them for us. It convicts, exposes, judges, and reveals the truth. If we want to find those hidden negative beliefs, we must read the Bible.

Allow the Holy Spirit to do His work and take time each day to read Scripture. Let your mind be washed with the Word. I love how Paul puts it in Colossians 3:16:

> Let the [spoken] word of Christ have its home within you [dwelling in your heart and mind—permeating every aspect of your being]. (AMP)

If you would've asked me a few years ago if I had rejection issues, I would've immediately and sincerely responded with a firm no. I had healthy self-esteem, my parents were still married, and I had a good group of trusted friends. I thought all those things checked the boxes and meant I didn't have any reason to deal with rejection. Though as I read the Bible and sat in His presence, the Holy Spirit started to confront me. Was I living *for* God's approval or *from* a place of love and acceptance?

The more I thought about it, the more I realized I often tried to earn God's love along with people's attention. My strong need for acceptance came from a place of rejection. Deep down I worried that maybe I wasn't loveable or worthy of attention. The funny part is, I didn't even realize I had this view until the Holy Spirit helped me unpack it.

Thankfully God gave me a new perspective, and I'm learning to see His love for what it is: unconditional and unending. I don't need to do anything to earn it.

God's Word changes our minds not because of our efforts but because of its power. The more we meditate on His Word, the more alive it becomes. We often think we must do XYZ to experience a dramatic change in our thoughts or feelings, but the Bible can do it for us. God's Word has the power to change our hearts and minds. When we wash ourselves in the Word and acknowledge Him in all we do, breakthrough is imminent. If you or your family wants to find lasting transformation, take time each day to read, meditate on, and memorize the Bible.

## Listen to the Words You Speak

The last thing you can do to transform your thought life is listen to the words you speak. Words reveal the thoughts and intents of the heart. For whatever comes out of the mouth comes from the heart (Matt. 15:18). Intentionally listen to the words you speak out loud to your husband, your children, your friends, and yourself. Pay attention to the words your children speak about themselves and others, for the mouth is the mirror of the heart. The mouth confesses what the heart believes. Is there any bitterness? Rudeness? Judgment? Gossip? The times I've intentionally paid attention to my words, I've been amazed and terrified by what I've learned.

Before we uproot any deep, dark thoughts, we first need to learn how to correctly identify them! Reflection is a valuable skill to master when learning to become emotionally healthy. We often want to rush the process and skip the reflection step because it takes work, vulnerability, and time. And what if we don't like what we see? Sometimes it's easier to lie to ourselves than be completely honest. Yet when we do this, we stay stuck.

Sound minds are born when we learn to accurately expose and express our most hidden thoughts. Because when we confront the lies, we conquer the darkness.

Don't allow those lies to stay in your mind a minute longer. Put them at God's feet, and as you ask Him to transform your mind, be more determined than ever to do the hard work.

**Brain Builder:** Take some time today to reflect on a recent time when you (or your child) felt stressed, anxious, or overwhelmed. What words did you (or they) speak? Our words reveal who we trust, the core beliefs we hold, and the lens through which we view the world. Can you identify any lies or misbeliefs you (or your child) believe based on the words you (or your child) often speak?

God can certainly heal our hearts and minds, but He can only restore what we surrender to Him. Give all your thoughts over to God. Stop fearing what's hidden in your mind. Seek God, confront the dark thoughts, and put on the mind of Christ. His mind is available to you and your children today. Are you actively seeking it?

# 5

# The Guard over Your Garden

Have you noticed how quick we as a society are to protect our possessions? We guard our homes by installing alarm systems. We guard our phones by setting passcodes. My family has even invested in extra protection against spills and toddler art for our couch. The majority of us worry about keeping our possessions safe and secure.

Last week I bought a small portable CD player for my kids. I love audiobooks because they keep children entertained without the use of a screen. I can enjoy my quiet time in the other room while the kids enjoy controlling the CD player in their room. It's a win-win for everyone. Although I intentionally showed my children how to use the player safely, within a week the antenna became bent and the top cracked. The kids owed my husband and me some of their chore money to cover the expense, but thankfully when I purchased the CD player, I also bought the extra protection plan. After a few emails, we got a replacement in the mail.

The incident in our house made me further question what we spend our time protecting. Our technology? Our fitness equipment? Our cars? If you think about it, almost everything we own worth over $500 has some type of protection, warranty, or safeguard. We intentionally protect our stuff.

Yet none of these things follow us to heaven. Wouldn't it make more sense to devote that time, energy, and intention to guarding the most valuable part of our physical being instead? We spent two chapters working hard to get our minds right. Let's not throw away that progress now by letting down our guard. We need to apply the same intention and care we use with our material possessions to protect our peace!

We read in Proverbs 4:23,

> Guard your heart above all else,
>    for it determines the course of your life. (NLT)

Is this something we do daily? What are we doing to protect our children's minds and hearts?

To better understand Scripture, I like looking up the Hebrew or Greek words of the original text. The Hebrew word for *guard* here in Proverbs means "to watch, to guard, to keep," and it's frequently used to express the idea of guarding or fortifying something, like a vineyard.[1] Vineyards and gardens must be protected to produce a bountiful harvest.

Additionally, the Hebrew word for *heart* here refers to the headquarters or the innermost being of a man or woman. The heart is a place where we store all our principles, thoughts, knowledge, feelings, and wisdom.[2] Our hearts and minds are intimately connected. In Scripture, "the heart" refers to the sum of our mind, emotions, and will.[3] Biblically speaking, we cannot separate the heart from the mind, and both must be protected.

Knowing the root meanings of the words, we can see that God doesn't say, "Hey, it might be a good idea to check in on your heart and mind every so often." He commands us to diligently protect and guard the innermost parts of our being. Why?

Because when our core is disrupted or broken, all the other systems fail.

## Who Are the Guardians?

Let's explore this idea of nurturing and guarding a garden. One day you go out to your garden box and sprinkle a few vegetable seeds in the dirt. You do nothing to prepare the soil, and you don't install any type of netting or fence. Instead, you pray for rain and hope for the best. When you walk out to your garden box in a few weeks, you find rabbits and slugs snacking on your lettuce and weeds taking over your box.

A few seeds grew and produced a small harvest without any intention or care, but it certainly wasn't bountiful. You think to yourself, *I should've put up a fence to protect the garden from unwanted intruders.* Why? Because the best-producing gardens are guarded.

Just like you need to nurture and protect your garden to produce good fruit, your mind also needs guarding. Thinking good thoughts isn't enough to build a sound mind. You need to build fences and keep careful watch to keep the pests out. Don't waste the time you spent pulling the stubborn weeds. You worked hard! Keep your sound mind by keeping guard.

## Jesus Is the Ultimate Guard

Part of protecting our sound minds is understanding that peace starts and ends with Jesus. We cannot lean on our own abilities to fix our thought life. As you work through this book, you may be tempted to think, *That's it. Deep breathing, a thought journal, or meditation is exactly what my kid needs. Now I have the tools to fix my child!* While science has given us great methods to soothe our stressed-out souls, true restoration and peace come only from God.

When seeking change, we play a crucial role in moving forward. We actively participate in the process of change. But transformation doesn't come through our efforts alone. Renewal isn't about trying harder; it's about surrendering it all to Jesus.

We fail every single time we try to conquer our minds in our own strength. We need help from above. Why not invite Him into the process? Our core Scripture for this chapter is found in Philippians 4:6–9, which says,

> Do not be anxious or worried about anything, but in everything [every circumstance and situation] by prayer and petition with thanksgiving, continue to make your [specific] requests known to God. And the peace of God [that peace which reassures the heart, that peace] which transcends all understanding, [that peace which] stands guard over your hearts and your minds in Christ Jesus [is yours].
>
> Finally, believers, whatever is true, whatever is honorable and worthy of respect, whatever is right and confirmed by God's word, whatever is pure and wholesome, whatever is lovely and brings peace, whatever is admirable and of good repute; if there is any excellence, if there is anything worthy of praise, think continually on these things [center your mind on them, and implant them in your heart]. The things which you have learned and received and heard and seen in me, practice these things [in daily life], and the God [who is the source] of peace and well-being will be with you. (AMP)

When we read this chapter in Philippians, we usually focus on the first part. Be honest. How many times have you heard a Christian say, "Be anxious for nothing"? We tell ourselves, "Just don't be anxious. You don't have anything to be worried about." But when we focus so much on trying not to be anxious, we end up feeling more anxious than when we started.

Meditating on not being fearful can backfire. We try to be fearless in our own strength when, in reality, we need Jesus to be fearless for us. When we focus on not worrying, we miss the promise tied to the end of this Scripture.

Let's take a closer look at the Greek word for *guard* in this verse. The Greek word here is *phroureo*, a military term that means to keep by guarding or to hem in and protect. "A watcher in advance."[4]

When we invite Jesus in, He stands at the gates of our hearts and minds watching. He's the ultimate guard to our inner beings. He sees our days in advance. As we pray and petition, we become anxious for nothing. Peace comes not by our willpower but by seeing a picture of Jesus standing guard over our lives. Then we are no longer anxious.

Right now, the Creator of the world desires to guard your heart and mind. Invite Him into your life by talking to Him daily. Bring all your cares, thoughts, worries, and concerns to Him through prayer. God wants to hear it all! I can't tell you how many times a day I speak out loud to Jesus. At first, my kids used to ask me, "Who are you talking to?" Now they know I'm talking either to myself or to Jesus.

When you lay your heart in Jesus's hands, He is faithful to protect it. What a beautiful image to see Jesus watching over your life by standing guard. He is the guard over your garden.

I love how the *Full Life Study Bible* describes this promise: "When we lay our troubles before God in prayer, this peace will stand guard at the doors of our hearts and minds, preventing the cares of life and the heartaches of disappointment from overthrowing our hope in Christ."[5]

## Parents Guard Their Kids

Parents play a significant role in building a hedge of protection around their children when they are young. Parents are the first guard in a child's life because, for the most part, they have control over the things their children see and hear. Childhood should be fun, free, and beautiful. But that doesn't mean parents shouldn't use discernment about the things their children consume.

A few years ago, our oldest daughter started reading a book series with a main character who is a major brat. The character talks back to her parents and teachers. And her friends think her misbehavior is funny. It's an extremely popular series for young readers, but after a few books, I noticed a change in our daughter's behavior. Instead of outlawing the books without explanation, I talked with our daughter about it. I explained to her how the things we read, watch, and listen to influence us whether we realize it or not. I asked her what she thought of the main character's behavior. She knew it wasn't appropriate. We didn't make a big deal about it, but we gently guided her to find a different series that would bring more life to her spirit.

Pay attention to what your children consume, guard their minds before they learn how to do this themselves. Also make sure when you set a boundary with your kids, you bring them into the conversation. Explain why you decided to limit a specific book or TV series. Certainly, there will be times when your children aren't happy about the boundaries you set. Likewise, other families in your neighborhood or community may not understand your decisions. In these times, it's essential to remember your why. We don't belong to this world, and the world hates us because of it (John 15:19). But God has called us higher. Stand firm in your convictions. What's the point of giving our kids pure water on Sunday if we allow dirt into the clean water throughout the week? Don't contaminate what God wants to do in your family's life!

Now, we can't move on from boundary setting without talking about screens. Electronics usage is a huge topic that's beyond the scope of this book. If you want to learn more about limiting screen usage, I recommend these two resources: *The Tech-Wise Family* and www.1000hoursoutside.com. It's getting harder and harder every day, but we must diligently monitor our children's screen time. I strongly recommend you hold off on giving your child a smartphone. I understand communication is important, but there are phones available now that don't have internet. Choose wisely!

I believe we must be intentional about monitoring screen usage, but we shouldn't live in fear about the age in which we live. Remember, you were born into this generation for a specific reason. God will equip you to parent your children with wisdom and discernment. Go back to Philippians 4:8 often and use it as a guide. Ask yourself, Does the movie, app, song, book, etc. line up with Scripture? Is it bringing life to our family?

## Parents Guard Themselves

We need to use the same level of scrutiny we apply to our children with the things we consume. Social media can distort our reality. Some days we just need a break from it all. We long to escape the piles of dirty laundry, the crying children who just won't take naps, and our boring, hard, exhausting lives. So we pick up our phones or turn on Netflix. Our minds find a moment of relief as we escape into someone else's life. But after a while, instead of feeling relaxed and rejuvenated, we step away from our phones feeling empty, lonely, and questioning why our lives aren't better. We start comparing our messy realities to someone else's highlight reel. It's a destructive cycle.

Don't even let yourself get there. Set up boundaries now to protect your mind, heart, and feelings. Your boundaries may look different from someone else's, and that's okay. You know your limits. You know what your family needs.

My family has turned on a movie we thought was okay, only to turn it off after a few minutes because it didn't sit well with us. Even if another family we respect recommended the movie, we decided to trust our gut.

Don't feel guilty or bad for saying no to something you know isn't right for your family. Listen to the Holy Spirit's promptings.

## Children as Little Guardians

As parents, we should protect our children from the dangers in this world. Along with that, our role as a guardian includes teaching our kids how to protect and guard their own hearts. We are our children's hedge, but at some point, we won't be around to filter out everything. We must give them the tools to guard their own hearts and minds even in our absence.

Kids can learn to listen to the Holy Spirit at a young age. I'll never forget the day we toured a potential home to buy. The first thing out of our five-year-old's mouth was "This house doesn't feel right." He was spot-on. We quickly walked past the Playboy pinball machine in the living room and tried to shield our children's eyes. Even with all the old farmhouse charm in the doorways and floors, the house felt dark. As we quickly exited the house, we encouraged our son to listen to the voice he'd heard that day. While adults typically have more wisdom than children, kids need to know that God can speak to them at a young age too. The more they pay attention to the Holy Spirit's leading, the better they'll be at hearing it. Nurture this skill in their little hearts.

Our oldest daughter loves to read, and while I try to preview books before I hand them over to her, sometimes I don't have time to read a novel a day to make sure it's safe. When I don't have time to read the entire text, I usually ask trusted friends their thoughts, do a quick google search, or look up the book on pluggedin.com. Somehow, I missed a chapter titled "A Ghost in the House" in the children's classic *Heidi*. Our daughter typically reads before bed, and one night she came into our room after we tucked her in to tell us the title of the next chapter. She asked if we could read it first because it made her feel uncomfortable. I felt awful that I had missed it, but as I read the chapter, I realized there wasn't really a ghost, just a sleepwalking child dressed in a white nightgown. Our daughter thought it was funny once I explained it to her, and then she continued to read.

Though that time the issue turned out to be innocent, I'm so grateful she came to us. It's important for children to look to their parents as the ultimate source of information. We've told our children over and over, "We will always tell you the truth. If it's something you need to know about, you can always come to us. No question is too silly." No matter how much we try to protect our children, kids talk. Inappropriate topics may come up, and it's extremely valuable for your children to feel comfortable enough to talk to you about them. Keep the communication open and encourage them to come to you with any and every question.

**Faith Former:** In Scripture, we see a young boy named Samuel hearing God's voice at night. Tonight read 1 Samuel 3 together as a family. Then discuss how even children can learn to discern God's voice. Children may not realize they can be used by God if we do not share this information with them.

We can help our children become guardians along with the Holy Spirit. God's Word promises that He'll pour out His spirit on our children (Joel 2:28). We shouldn't take this promise lightly. We can help our children hear God's voice and learn how to respond to the Spirit's promptings by taking time each week to listen for the Lord's voice. For our family, this looks like singing a few worship songs and then sitting in reflection. After a few minutes, we encourage the kids to share if they heard anything from God. It could be a phrase, a Bible verse that comes to memory, or an image they may have seen in their heads. It takes practice, but kids can learn to hear God's voice at a young age.

## Guarding by Thinking Lovely Thoughts

Now that we know who the guardians are, we need to learn the best ways to guard. Paul instructs us in Philippians to think of lovely things. If we want to experience the peace of God, we must align our hearts and minds with honorable, pure, excellent thoughts.

The other day I was driving when my son requested a specific song from his Sonic video game to listen to. My husband grew up liking Sonic, so I believed the music was acceptable. As I started listening to some of the lyrics, I felt a stirring in my spirit. The words in this specific song didn't bring life and light; instead, they focused on darkness and pain. I told my kids we had to turn the song off. Immediately I heard grumbling and saw eye-rolling in the rearview mirror. "But why? I want to listen to it," my son said.

Car rides seem to be ripe for teaching moments in our family. I shared with my kids how the Bible instructs us to think of lovely, pure, and excellent things. I asked them if the lyrics from the Sonic song lined up with that Scripture.

They knew the answer was no, but in the rearview mirror I could see their minds working through it. At first, they hesitated to answer because they wanted to listen to the song. Their hearts experienced a clash between culture and kingdom.

I sympathized with their wrestling hearts. I explained how there are times when I'm watching a show and I feel that same nudge. *Maybe you shouldn't be watching this, Lauren. Is this really edifying you?* Part of me wants to ignore that voice because I'm enjoying the show, plus everyone else is watching it. But the Holy Spirit is talking to me, and I need to listen because He instructs us with wisdom from heaven.

Though my kids initially moaned, they learned a valuable lesson that day. We need to wisely choose what our eyes see, what our hearts hear, and what our minds meditate on. While Jesus stands at the gate of our minds, we have the power to tell Him to move. Because we have free will, He allows us to open the gate. The Holy Spirit will always warn us, but we can ignore those warnings and allow those intruders in anyway.

We wonder why we don't have peace, why we feel anxious, and why we can't sleep well at night. But then we turn on the TV and watch depressing news or listen to music filled with heartache, negativity, and haughtiness. The Bible clearly tells us in Philippians that the meditations of our minds matter. While certain shows, songs, or movies may seem harmless initially, when we allow death in, it'll destroy our harvest. We need to ask ourselves, What are we allowing into our minds? Our spirits? What seeds are we sowing? What is germinating? Don't intentionally let the intruder in through the front gate. Protect your peace!

God intentionally sets two paths before each one of us: one filled with earthly treasure that temporarily satisfies but eventually rots and decays and another filled with overflowing, eternal blessing. In Deuteronomy 30:19, we read, "I call heaven and earth as witnesses today against you, that I have set before you life and death, blessing and cursing; therefore choose life, that both you and your descendants may live."

How do we choose life? By guarding our mouths and our hearts. Deuteronomy 30:14 tells us, "But the word is very near you, in your mouth and in your heart, that you may do it." The ideas your heart focuses on influence the road you choose. The meditations of your mind influence your everyday actions. Guard them diligently! Why? Because the mind controlled by carnal thoughts leads to death. Paul tell us in Romans 8:6,

Now the mind of the flesh is death [both now and forever—because it pursues sin]; but the mind of the Spirit is life and peace [the spiritual well-being that comes from walking with God—both now and forever]. (AMP)

Alternatively, the mind focused on following Jesus leads to life. Build that fence. Protect your house. Choose life. That you and your descendants may live.

## Guarding by Taking First Thoughts Captive

We uprooted some weeds—unhelpful thoughts—in chapter 4. And in this chapter, we've learned how to guard our gardens— our innermost beings—and now we need to plant new, healthy seeds—healthy thoughts. Mind renewal starts first thing in the morning.

This Brain Builder is an excellent practice for keeping our minds healthy. Kids can learn to take their first thoughts captive too. Our first thoughts set our heart posture for the day. I notice a huge difference when I wake up and say, "Thank You, Jesus, for this day. Thank You for the breath in my lungs" compared to moaning, "Ugh, I don't want to get up. I'm so tired. I'm always tired." When my thoughts start out negatively, they only continue to spiral from there. Before my feet even hit the ground, my thoughts can either taint or brighten the day. If we want a transformed mind, we must get ahold of our first thoughts. Refuse to start your day with anything anxious, negative, or self-defeating.

**Brain Builder:** Tomorrow when you wake up in the morning, I want you to try to capture the first thought you think. Write it down in the margin of this book or in a notebook next to your bed. Then ask yourself, Was my first thought filled with life or death? How did this set the tone for my day?

Along with capturing our first thoughts, we should take intentional time every day to sit still in His presence, meditating on the good. Pondering God's truth. Life is busy, and often if we don't do this first thing in the morning, we won't get to it. Make it a priority to get your mind centered before heading out the door. And while I love a good devotional, something about God's Word cuts through all the mess and brings renewal to our minds. Pick up your Bible.

Ideally, we should be meditating on God's Word day and night. For we read in Joshua 1:8, "Study this Book of Instruction continually. Meditate on it day and night so you will be sure to obey everything written in it. Only then will you prosper and succeed in all you do" (NLT). Cultivate your children's minds and anchor them in God's truth by aiming to read His word together every day.

Now, before you start figuring out how to run a formal Bible study in your living room every night, hear me out. While it's wonderful to study His Word with your family, casual conversations like the one I had in the car over music can be just as powerful. Seek to bring God's Word into your day-to-day occurrences. The more you meditate on His Word, the more alive it becomes to you and the easier it will be to see Him move throughout your day.

## Guarding by Understanding the Heart-Mind Connection

We have guardians, and they actively guard because there's a heart-mind connection. As you've seen in this chapter, our hearts and minds are closely related. Our thoughts slowly penetrate down into our hearts. The effect starts small, but over time one bad thought turns into a persistent belief that impacts our daily actions. Our actions influence our core values, which determine the course of our lives. Can you see how one little thought makes a significant impact?

This idea is powerful because it shows the cascade effect of bad thinking. That's why we spent three chapters learning how to take control of our thoughts. When a child learns to protect their mind, they guard themselves against attacks of the enemy. Because typically an attack from our adversary starts in the mind. If he wins the battle in our minds, then bitterness, discouragement, and defeat take up residence in our hearts. The enemy deceives us through our minds because he knows our thoughts lead the way to our innermost being. The mind talks to the heart. This is what I call the top-down process of the heart-mind connection. Simultaneously, a bottom-up process is happening. The heart also speaks to the mind. We read in multiple Scripture verses that to know what's in our hearts, all we need to do is start listening to our words.

For out of the abundance of the heart his mouth speaks. (Luke 6:45)

But those things which proceed out of the mouth come from the heart. (Matt. 15:18)

Our mouths reveal to us what's deeply seeded within our hearts. I love how the *New Spirit-Filled Life Bible* sums up the heart-mind connection: "Oral confession declares, confirms and seals the belief in the heart."[6] Negative oral confession reveals a discouraged or disappointed heart. However, a person joyfully confessing the goodness of God reveals a healthy heart.

In the following chapters, we'll inspect our hearts for wounds or sin. As we move on, I want us to think about the words we're speaking and the thoughts we're meditating on throughout the day. What insight are those thoughts giving us about our perspectives and beliefs? Do any narratives need to change? Get ready, because we're about to dive deep into the thoughts and intents of our hearts.

# 6

# Our Walls Have Scars

As I wrote this week, a handyman pounded and sanded our foyer walls, covering a massive gash in the drywall as well as multiple dents and nicks.

A few months ago, to celebrate our twelfth anniversary, we bought our first couch. Thankfully through the years we've been blessed with couches from other people. While the couches have been great, there's something special about picking out a new piece of furniture that's exactly your taste, you know what I mean? I was giddy at the furniture store when we chose one with a chaise lounge. We waited four months, and the day had finally come! Soon I'd be lounging on the couch of my dreams.

At 6:00 p.m., the doorbell rang. As I walked to the front door, I saw the delivery truck in our driveway. The men brought in the first piece through the front door as I stood by anxiously waiting to see the beautiful couch. As they neared the basement door, I saw a look of concern on the lead guy's face. The couch wouldn't fit through the basement doorframe. "No problem," he said. "We can just take off the legs." After forty-five minutes of trying their best to maneuver the couch—the one I'd been waiting twelve years for—they told me they'd have to come back the next day with a different set of tools.

Sadly, the chaise lounge wouldn't fit, so we had to cancel the entire order. It wasn't until the delivery truck pulled out of our driveway that we noticed the huge hole in the ceiling and the marks on the wall. We ended up with no couch and a few wounded walls. That wasn't the first time we'd had to repaint and repair dents and marks on our walls, and it certainly won't be the last. But hopefully, I won't have to wait another twelve years to get my dream couch.

As the handyman repaired our broken walls, I thought about the wounds, scars, and gashes we collect throughout our lives. The ones that cut deep enough to impact our hearts. The ones that leave lasting marks. While everyone's scars look different, we all have them. The question is, What are we doing about them?

It's time to inspect the heart growth area. While teaching your child how to read or ride a bike is an important part of childhood development, I'd argue that shepherding a child's heart is the *most* important. For the heart is the center of it all. The heart holds our core beliefs and houses our innermost being. In Proverbs 27:19, we read,

> As in water face reflects face,
> So a man's heart reveals the man.

Life flows from our hearts, revealing what the deepest parts of us think, feel, and believe. Our hearts contain the essence of who we are, so it makes sense that we should take care of them.

Unfortunately, we live in a fallen world, and because of this, our hearts will sustain wounds from the journey. Too many of us walk around with distressed and wounded hearts. We're broken and battered, and we're missing out on God's abundant grace because of it. I'm here to tell you today that God cares too deeply for us to leave us broken. He wants to restore our souls and bring complete health and healing to our innermost beings. Jesus came to proclaim freedom and liberty to the captives (Luke 4:16–21). Our wounds no longer have to hold us captive; we can find freedom in Jesus today. Heart healing is a worthy endeavor, because it will not only restore our souls but also transform how we parent.

## The Twist

Here's that twist again. Before we can shepherd our children's hearts well and make sure they are whole, we first need to inspect our own. We can more effectively nurture our children's hearts when we care for and tend to the wounds, sins, and lies lingering within ours. Right now, I wish I could be sitting across from you at a kitchen table with a cup of coffee in hand. I'd love to be with you as I bring up this next topic because I'm not going to sugarcoat it: heart healing can hurt.

I wish you could hear my tone of voice right now as I tell you it's going to be okay. How do I know this? Because God promised.

> He heals the brokenhearted
> and binds up their wounds. (Ps. 147:3 NIV)

With God's help, you *can* confront the hard stuff, break generational patterns, overcome sin, and pull down strongholds.

Uncovering these areas may be uncomfortable. Some of our perspectives that need to change can be hard to see at first, and we may not want to open past wounds. My goal isn't to have you sit in grief, pain, or trauma forever. On the other side of your pain is freedom, hope, peace, and joy. You don't have to carry those heavy hurts around with you forever. You can feel light. You can live in freedom through Jesus. When it feels too hard, keep pushing through the pain, sadness, and sin so you can find rest for your soul.

As you read this chapter, my prayer is that you will have the courage to care for your wounded heart and confront your sins, because recognizing the state of your heart is an essential step toward finding wholeness. And whole parents raise wholesome kids.

## Two Heart Areas

In this chapter, we'll challenge two areas of the heart. The first is heart wounds. I wish it weren't true, but we live in a fallen world. A world filled with sin and brokenness. This means bad things happen to good people, and in our journeys, we'll collect both intentional and unintentional wounds. Through my years on this earth, I've collected a handful myself—a few of which I'd love to ignore. But I know that if I hold on to my wounds, it only limits me from seeing more of God's goodness in my life.

The second area is sin. While we strive to live more righteous lives, all of us are born with self-serving hearts, and that means we'll have to deal with sin. When we don't address sin in our lives, it brings destruction. Wounds and sin greatly impact our hearts, which influence the way we parent.

## What Is a Wound?

When we talk about healing, I don't mean physical ailments— though I believe God wants to heal those too. In this section, we're addressing heart wounds, or places in our innermost being that've been hurt or damaged by another person, event, or experience. Heart wounds come in all shapes and sizes. Every wound hurts and needs gentle care to heal completely, but some wounds need more attention and love than others.

It upsets me to think that some of us are walking around with trauma from sexual, physical, or emotional abuse or from a loved one dying unexpectedly or from a terrifying diagnosis. These are deep wounds. For deep wounds, it's best to work through the pain with a trained and licensed professional. Seeking extra help for your heart is a brave thing to do. The journey may be painful, but the freedom waiting for you on the other side is worth it.

While not everyone has deep wounds to work through, all of us suffer from small gashes and scrapes that impact our lives. Has someone ever made an off-the-cuff comment that stung a little more than you expected? Or have you experienced a friendship slowly ending? These experiences still influence our hearts.

Wounds can be sneaky because we may not realize their impact until we stop and reflect on them. I have often thought to myself, *I've already dealt with that. I'm ready to move on.* But as I spent more time in prayer and reflection, I realized I wasn't completely healed and a wound remained in my heart. Because of my busy life, I had been able to avoid confronting the pain. The same issues kept coming up, and when I finally paid attention, I realized I needed to deal with them. If the same problems keep arising in your life, it may be time to inspect further.

## How to Address Our Wounds

While I believe inner healing is not only important but also possible, I'm hesitant to give you specific prompts to receive healing. Why? Because there is no secret formula. God moves in miraculous ways. I've experienced His intimate touch when I was alone with Him in the secret place (Matt. 6:6), and I've also experienced His healing hand when I was at a worship event with other believers. I've experienced Matthew 18:20 in real time with small prayer groups: "For where two or three are gathered together in My name, I am there in the midst of them." In this section, I could provide you with specific scripts or activities to say or do this or that, but ultimately healing comes from God, not from my words.

That being said, God is sovereign. He can use my words and what I share with you about inner healing to increase your faith. And because of your faith, God moves on your behalf. As you read this chapter, remember this: God's ways are higher than our own, and while there's no magic formula, there are three biblical principles you can follow to search your heart and draw you closer to Jesus, who was whipped for your healing (Isa. 53:5).

### 1. Acknowledge Christ

The first biblical principle related to inner healing is acknowledging that Jesus Christ is Lord. If we want freedom, Jesus is the person to give it to us. True freedom comes only from Him. To access His redemptive power, we must confess with our mouths that Jesus is Lord and believe in our hearts that God raised Him from the dead (Rom. 10:9). To see God as our healer, we must acknowledge He is Lord over it all (Eph. 4:6). No one is higher or greater than Jesus. God has lifted Him up and given Him the name that is above every name (Phil. 2:9). Jesus's highest position gives Him the authority to restore whatever He wants to restore, and there's nothing too broken for Him to fix.

After we acknowledge Christ is over everything, we can move on to the second principle. This is where we get in God's presence. If you walk away from this chapter with anything, I want it to be this: God's presence brings the deepest healing.

### 2. Search the Heart

I grew up in a Christian home, but I didn't become comfortable praying out loud for a long time. I often heard people say to "invite the Holy Spirit in" and "practice His presence," but I didn't exactly know what they meant until I took a leap of faith and started talking aloud to Jesus. If you want to learn how to practice being in His presence, you must find a quiet place to be alone with God. We hear about the secret place in Psalm 91:1:

**Faith Former:** Find a quiet room, away from distractions, where you can talk to Jesus. It's as simple as saying, "Holy Spirit, come. Make yourself known to me. Holy Spirit, you are my helper, and you can teach me all things [John 14:26]. As I sit in your presence today, bring me revelation and wisdom. Show me the depths of God's love and open my eyes to see things the way You do. In Jesus's name, amen." Take time to sit with God. Ask Him to search your heart, and see if He shows you any areas that need healing.

> He who dwells in the secret place of the Most High
> Shall abide under the shadow of the Almighty.

If we want to rest under God's wings, we need to get into that secret place.

God wants you to ask, seek, and knock. Go to His throne and share your heart with Him. It really is that simple. Another way to usher in the Holy Spirit's presence and experience God's healing hand is through praise. The Bible tells us God inhabits the praises of His people (Ps. 22:3). You can praise God alone in your secret place, in a small group, or in a large congregation. Any way you do it, it is a practice you'll want to do often. The *New Spirit-Filled Life Bible* puts it perfectly: "Few principles are more essential to our understanding than this one: the <u>presence</u> of God's kingdom power is directly related to the practice of God's <u>praise</u>."[1]

If you've never prayed out loud before or danced around your room in praise, it may be awkward the first few times you do it. Hearing God's voice can feel like this mystical, magical thing, but we often make it more complex than it needs to be. We get into His presence by praying and praising. And when we slow down and practice being in His presence, we begin to hear His voice.

As you spend time with God, ask Him to search your heart. Jeremiah 17:10 tells us,

> I, the LORD, search the heart,
> I test the mind.

God will gently reveal the wounds that need to be healed, and He will show you where the wound originated. David knew this when he prayed in Psalm 139:23–24,

> Search me, God, and know my heart;
>     test me and know my anxious thoughts.
> See if there is any offensive way in me,
>     and lead me in the way everlasting. (NIV)

Follow David's example. Ask God to search your heart and lead you to the truth. Allow Him to reveal the depths of your heart to you. Healing may be instantaneous or it may take time as God slowly transforms your innermost parts. If healing doesn't happen immediately, don't fret. God is still on the throne. Keep seeking His face. If you feel like you need to invite someone into the process, talk to a trusted friend or family member who can pray with you.

Heart wounds can be extremely difficult to relive, and facing the pain alone can be unbearable. Personal prayer is only one way to receive healing. If reading this section makes you feel like you need more help processing the trauma or pain, I highly recommend talking to your pastor, finding a professional counselor, or seeking out a prayer ministry in your area. It's always wise to find trusted people to walk through the healing journey with you. You are brave for seeking professional help, and alleviating the pain is a worthy endeavor.

### 3. Confrontation and Radical Forgiveness

The last biblical principle we'll look at related to wounds is confrontation and radical forgiveness. We serve a mighty God, but at times sin separates us from His power and leaves us with wounds. It's important to note that not all heart wounds occur because of personal sin. At times wounds occur because of other people's sins. We had nothing to do with the trauma. It's important to discern the difference. If our wounds were caused by personal sin, we need to confront it. Did the Holy Spirit bring anything to your mind while you sat in His presence? All of us have sinned and fallen short of the glory of God (Rom. 3:23), but thankfully that's not the end of the story. God sent His one and only Son to pay the ultimate price for our sin (John 3:16). Because of this gift, when we confess our sin, He's faithful to forgive us and bring us back into right standing with Him (1 John 1:9).

If some else's sin caused our wounds, we also have to address it—but in a different way. Forgiveness could mean offering grace to someone who doesn't deserve it or making a conscious decision to let go of past pains caused by another person. Forgiving someone who hurt you so deeply can feel impossible. I can't imagine the heartache some of you have experienced because of someone else's behavior. It doesn't seem fair, but this is what I know: Jesus instructs us to forgive those who hurt us (Matt. 18:21–22). And unforgiveness damages us more than anyone else. It can prevent us from receiving freedom, and it limits our communication with God. Forgiveness can take time. If you need more help with forgiveness, I highly recommend reading Lysa TerKeurst's *Forgiving What You Can't Forget*, in which she walks you through the steps of radical forgiveness.

We walk in a fallen world, and our hearts will collect a few nicks, gashes, and holes, but no wound is too deep for God to mend. As we seek healing, we may never forget the mark, but it doesn't have to cause us anguish or annoyance any longer.

## When Hard Times Come

I recently went through a time of healing. The wound I worked through came from an experience I had over twenty years ago. At my sixth-grade physical, the doctor noticed a slight curve in my spine. He said the curve was minimal but suggested I see a specialist. A few months later, the specialist gave me a full torso brace to wear for twenty-three hours a day. Every few months, I went back to the doctor, who looked to see if the brace had worked to slow my spine's curve. Unfortunately, my curve kept getting worse. Each time we received the disappointing news, my family and I cried.

We prayed and prayed that God would heal my back and I wouldn't need surgery to stop the curve from progressing. My mom's entire side of the family laid hands on me and prayed. We'd never done anything like that before, yet we believed God could provide healing. Despite all our prayers, on May 5, 1999, doctors wheeled me into an operating room to perform a five-hour surgery that changed my life.

At the age of thirteen, I underwent scoliosis reconstruction surgery. Two rods were placed along my spine to reduce the curve by fusing my vertebrae into a straighter place. I struggled for the next year as I tried to get back to normal life. Most of my friends moved on as I did school at home for a few months. As a thirteen-year-old girl, the loss of friendship devastated me.

I also swam competitively, and the winter before my surgery, I'd won third place in the fifty-yard freestyle at Junior Olympics. After the surgery, I had to swim with kids half my age as I regained my strength. I wasn't allowed to dive off the blocks for a full year and often fought thoughts of *Why me God? Bad things only happen to me.* I eventually found my groove again, won a gold medal in a relay at state, and birthed three nine-pound babies without any pain management. Because of my perceived success, I thought I'd overcome all the hurt and pain. Years later, I realized heaviness remained in my heart from that traumatic event.

Another unexpected health issue finally forced me to confront the deep wound. At first, I didn't connect the dots that wounds from the past could still affect my current emotional health. I had a master's in psychology, and I'd convinced myself I knew how to handle stress. For years I'd written about holding every thought captive. Surely stress or unresolved trauma wasn't my problem.

Though as time went on and I started digging through my thought life, I realized a lot of my doubts and questions stemmed from that significant event in my life. No matter how much I tried to tell myself, *Be brave Lauren,* I still questioned, *Does the God of the universe care for me? And if He does, then why am I dealing with sickness and disease?*

Even typing out this story, tears formed in my eyes. I love God so much, and I believe His Word is true. But I'd be lying if I didn't say the enemy has tried to make me question God's faithfulness and love on several occasions. The surgery being a big one.

When bad things happen, we often want to blame God and ask why He would allow such heartache. The devil wants us to question and doubt every promise of God. That's why it's so important to know His Word. When Jesus was tempted in the desert, He didn't overcome Satan's testing by praying or dancing or stomping. He did it by declaring and speaking God's Word with authority. During challenging seasons, we must remember that Jesus came to give us life and life more abundantly (John 10:10). Wherever Jesus went, He brought life and health.

Talking with trusted friends and counselors and praying and reading my Bible brought me to a place of healing. In my journey, I also used Dr. Caroline Leaf's Neurocycle App to help rewire my brain. I enjoyed her app daily as it took me step-by-step through the rewiring process. I intentionally changed my thoughts and healed my heart, but that doesn't mean I don't still remember the pain. While I've heard people say God completely removed memories from their brains (and I believe He can do that), for me, the memories remain—but now I see God in them.

Friend, healing and freedom are available to you also. Allow God to gently mend the wounds on the walls of your heart. The discomfort of facing painful memories is worth the wholeness Jesus has for you waiting on the other side.

## Confronting Our Sin

Another barrier to having a healed heart is sin. It's always a bit uncomfortable talking about sin, isn't it? But it's a conversation worth having because sin separates us from God. Sin breaks relationships and distorts truth. Sin leads to death (James 1:15). Whether or not we want to admit it, when sin is present in our lives it doesn't just hurt us, it hurts our spouses and our kids. So, if we want to raise emotionally healthy children, we can't avoid this talk.

Sin is sneaky, and it's often easier to see it in someone else's life before we spot it in our own. But we'll never be free of it if we don't learn to confront it. That may mean forgiving the person who hurt you so deeply, repenting for idolizing money and success, or asking for forgiveness for coveting and lusting over the big, luxurious houses you see on Instagram. When you ask God to search your heart, He may point out some wounds He wants to heal, but He also may point out some motives He wants to change. We must confront our sin head-on, confess it, and then walk in the other direction.

Sometimes it feels easier to run from our sin or pretend it isn't happening. But the Bible tells us over and over again how God will bring every act to judgment, even those that are hidden (Eccles. 12:14; Luke 12:2). In time, everything will be revealed. You can't run from your sin. Take care of lingering sin now before it becomes a more significant issue.

Though God despises sin, thankfully He's faithful to cleanse us from all unrighteousness. Repenting from sin cleans our hearts and allows us to walk in freedom. The catch is, we first must admit it to Him. We read in 1 John 1:9, "If we confess our sins, He is faithful and just to forgive us our sins and to cleanse us from all unrighteousness." While we were born with self-serving hearts, God can transform that part of us. And by allowing the Spirit to work in our hearts and lead us away from our fleshly desires, our hearts become renewed and we become more stable and available parents for our children.

Children benefit from parents who model how to confront sin. It can be helpful for our children to see us repent of our sins in front of them. Obviously we need to use discretion. For example, if the sin is lust or drunkenness, we probably shouldn't pray openly about it in front of our children. Other sins, like anger, may be more appropriate to share. Let's say we got angry with our children and yelled at them unnecessarily. We realize

 **How to Confront Sin in Our Children**

- First, we should remind our children what sin is by asking, "What is sin?" Answer: "Sin is an intentional act of wrongdoing. It is not a mistake or accident. It's a purposeful decision to rebel against God."

- Then we can ask our children, "What you just did, would you qualify that as a sin?" At this point, hopefully, they're able to recognize their sin. If they can't see their actions as sinful, I recommend reading what Scripture says about the behavior. In appendix A, you'll find Scripture references for the most common childhood sins to help you get started.

- Lastly, "What does the Bible tell us to do if we sin?" Read James 5:16 together: "Therefore confess your sins to each other and pray for each other so that you may be healed" (NIV). Also read 1 John 1:9, "If we confess our sins, he is faithful and just and will forgive us our sins and purify us from all unrighteousness" (NIV). Then take time to pray together. Our children should confess their sin, then ask Jesus for forgiveness.

- During the discussion, we must make sure our children understand that what they did was wrong, but our love for them hasn't changed.

we were wrong, so we ask for their forgiveness. We can use this experience to invite them into our prayer. It could sound something like this: "God, please forgive me for yelling at my children today. I felt frustrated and let it get the best of me. I'm sorry for allowing anger to control my emotions. Thank you for cleansing my heart. In Jesus's name, amen." When we model prayers of confession in front of our children, we give them a guide for how to do the same when they sin.

There will be times when we need to confront our children's sins. Though this can feel unpleasant, it's something we as parents need to get comfortable doing.

A sin many families with young children deal with is lying. A few weeks ago, my friend shared a situation that sounded like something that would happen in our house. Her kids were playing outside as she prepped dinner. At one point her youngest son came in soaking wet, crying, and saying his sister sprayed him in the face. As soon as the older child heard his accusations, she replied, "No, I didn't!" Though, clearly, my friend could see the little boy's face dripping with water and the hose in the other child's hand. It didn't take long for her to put two and two together and realize one of her children had lied. The child had meant to say, "I didn't do it on purpose," but instead of fessing up to the mistake, the child chose to save face and lie. Making a mistake isn't a problem, but lying about it is.

Sometimes the lie seems innocent. While the saying "White lies don't hurt anyone" is popular, the truth is that lying is never good. In these moments, we must confront our children and explain that lying is a sin that hurts not only God but also other people. Everyone makes mistakes, and grace should be a big part of our homes. However, when we see purposeful disobedience in our children, we need to address it.

Sin is a part of our world, but Jesus is the answer to this problem. Our children need to know they don't have to live under condemnation. We don't have to keep making the same mistakes.

Jesus tells us to go and sin no more (John 8:11). We can walk in the other direction and live a life of freedom.

## Take Care of Yourself First

Now, I know you care deeply for your child's heart. Otherwise, you wouldn't be reading this book. But don't forget to take care of yourself first. The enemy wants you to walk around wounded. Then you'll never become the fierce, strong parent God created you to be. Wounds, sins, and lies don't come from our Heavenly Father. Wherever Jesus went, He brought light, life, freedom, and wholeness. God promises abundance for you. Take a step today to walk toward it. Don't let lingering wounds or sin remain in your heart.

# 7

# Winning Your Child's Heart

I still remember the day our oldest daughter tried the monkey bars for the first time. We visited a local park, and as the kids played, I stood off to the side observing. The kids tried different activities and eventually ended up near the monkey bars. My daughter's friend went across first, and as she swung from bar to bar, I saw determination in my daughter's eyes. She wanted to try it herself.

She stepped up and took the first leap. Her legs flailed from side to side as she moved her hands cautiously from one brightly colored bar to the next. As she neared the end, a huge smile swept across her face. She let go, and as soon as her feet hit the ground, she looked around and started yelling, "Mom! Mom! I just did the monkey bars!"

My heart leapt. It made me so happy to see her succeed. Even more heartwarming was the fact that she wanted to share this moment with *me*. She didn't know I'd watched her the entire time. It's these little moments in parenthood that melt away the cares of the world—the huge smile when your child steps off the school bus and sees you waiting, the swell in your heart as you watch them sleep. Moments when your heart deeply connects with theirs.

The deep heart connections we form with our children make all the challenges, struggles, and ups and downs of parenting worthwhile. In this chapter, we'll learn why winning our children's hearts matters and how to intentionally cultivate this type of connection. The heart bond we build with our children is a beautiful part of parenthood.

## Why Winning Our Children's Hearts Matters

We are our children's first role models. The routines and rhythms we build into our families, as well as our expectations and responses, impact our children's hearts and brains forever. The National Association for the Education of Young Children explains early childhood relationships this way: "The relationships a child experiences each day and the environments in which those relationships play out are the building blocks of the brain."[1] When we win our children's hearts, we establish firm foundations for their emotional and spiritual development.

Research tells us that children who form secure attachments with their parents early on are later rated by their teachers as higher in self-esteem and empathy and are seen as more socially competent compared to their insecurely attached counterparts.[2] How amazing is it that the parent-child relationship impacts present and future growth? Don't wait to nurture your child's heart. The relationship you intentionally build and cultivate with them now will have a ripple effect for years to come.

When you establish healthy heart connections, you equip your child with the skills to live happy, well-adjusted lives. According to researchers, healthy family relationships provide kids with the tools to better cope with stress and engage in healthier behaviors, which lead to overall higher well-being.[3] Who doesn't want that for their child?

Now, as you read this chapter, I don't want you to start thinking you have to get it all perfect to have a healthy relationship with your child. The National Center on Parenting, Family, and Community Engagement gives excellent advice on this aspect of parenting: "Parents do not have to be perfectly attuned to their child at every moment, nor do they need to respond perfectly to each of the child's cues. Regular, sensitive responses whenever possible are enough."[4] Don't put unnecessary pressure on yourself to respond perfectly to every social interaction with your child. You don't need to make all the right decisions to build a healthy heart connection with your child.

## Three Keys to Winning Your Child's Heart

Okay, we know it's essential to create a loving, secure attachment with our child, but how do we do this? There are three keys to winning your child's heart: creating "I love you" moments, eating meals together, and establishing healthy communication.

### 1. Find "I Love You" Moments

Quality time is my love language, so hanging out with my people is where my heart prospers. It's worthwhile to prioritize quality time with your kids, even if it's not your top method of giving or receiving love. I always encourage parents to find special "I love you" moments with their kids throughout the day. These moments occur when we're intentionally present and recognize the value of heart-to-heart connection. Moments when we share our favorite part of the day, hug each other for longer than ten seconds, and put the phone down and chat honestly while looking each other in the eyes.

There have been nights when I've realized I haven't spent one moment of the entire day intentionally listening to and looking at my children as they spoke. Then I felt terrible that I'd let the busyness of life prevent me from spending quality time with the people I love. Of course, life is busy, and kids always seem to want to talk at the most inconvenient times, like when we're cooking dinner, answering an email, or speaking to another adult. But is that a valid excuse? It appears we as a society have lost the art of looking each other in the eyes. I'm not talking about looking at someone for a few seconds to acknowledge you are listening. I mean actual eye contact, where we focus on what the person is saying without any distractions around us.

**Faith Former:** How often do you spend quality one-on-one time with your family members? How many times a day do you hit that little Instagram or Facebook icon to scroll and "see what's happening"? Take an honest look at your daily interactions. Does anything need to change? Try to find at least one "I love you" moment today with your children.

God created us to be in relationships. When we're in thriving relationships, a deep need is fulfilled within us. We must guard this, because in today's world we have so many things striving for our attention. We need to be intentional, or we can quickly lose these face-to-face connections. Our society is overworked, and it's not good for our kids' hearts or minds. We need to find time each day to truly engage with them.

I get it, sometimes life as a parent is boring. I don't find packing lunches, playing pretend, and chauffeuring kids around all that exciting, but that fact shouldn't give me the go-ahead to entertain and distract myself with my phone. We need to find healthier ways to cope with the mundane and boring parts of parenthood. Relationships shouldn't be put on the back burner because we struggle to connect with each other in meaningful ways.

A few years ago, I heard someone say they have "date nights" with their child every month, and I thought it was an excellent idea. Because the child was born on October 1, every first of the month the parent scheduled a special date night for them and their child. They would do something, such as go to Starbucks for a treat or take a bike ride together around the neighborhood. It didn't have to be fancy, but the schedule kept them accountable for spending quality time with their child.

I'm not advocating that we entertain and engage with our children all day, every day. That's not practical or realistic. At times kids need to learn how to entertain themselves. Boredom is good for them, and it's okay for them to learn that parents aren't available every hour of the day. But we can't let our adult responsibilities take us away from the most precious gifts of all: our children. There has to be a balance between work—whether it's outside the house or inside as a stay-at-home mom—and family. To build deep heart connections, we must find time to be together and enjoy one another's company.

## 2. Prioritize Family Dinner

If you're looking for ways to connect with your child on a deeper level, family dinner is one of the best ways to do it. I'm a huge advocate of regular family dinners, where you deliberately turn off the screens and engage in real conversation with one another. It's not easy with everyone's schedules, and dinnertime seems to be particularly crazy in our house with three small kids. On the days when everyone is arguing and getting up from their seats while I'm trying to have a calm conversation with my family, I try to remind myself of the benefits of shared family meals.

### FAMILY DINNER BUILDS FAITH

Eating dinner together is a chance to build your children's faith. According to Barna, vibrant households are more likely to spend quality time together having fun.[5] This includes eating meals together. Families who did a good job building a foundation of faith ate together—75 percent ate dinner together and 63 percent ate breakfast together.[6] Mealtime is an opportunity

113

to connect. When you sit and remove distractions, you have an opportunity to share real-life examples of how God is moving in your life, which builds children's faith.

### FAMILY DINNER IS PROTECTIVE

In addition to the opportunity to connect and engage with your children, family dinners benefit the whole child. Research suggests that eating family meals together boosts a child's physical and emotional well-being. In addition to having higher grade point averages and spending more time on homework and reading for pleasure, children who eat meals with their families are less likely to experiment with tobacco, alcohol, and marijuana.[7] Make sharing meals a priority now so that when life gets busy, it's already an established routine in your home. Family dinner gives you a chance to enjoy one another's company and share the joys and pains of life together.

I know eating dinner together feels impossible for some families. With my husband's unpredictable work schedule, I under-

 **Practical Tips for Mealtimes**

- Have everyone put their phones in a time-out spot during family time. Then you won't be tempted to start scrolling or feel the need to immediately respond to nonurgent messages.

- Share your wins with your family. Kids love hearing about your day. Use these experiences to show them how God moved in your life.

- Don't be afraid to share your challenges with your family. Celebrate the wins, but also be transparent and share the struggles, frustrations, and challenges. We all go through trials. Teach your kids how to be courageous and move forward in their battles by sharing the ways you overcome challenges.

stand this frustration. But it's worth asking yourself and your family, What can we do to change our schedules and prioritize dinner together? Sometimes things are out of our control, but other times we *can* change something; it's just a matter of whether we *want* to change. Changing your schedule probably won't be convenient, and it may mean saying no to things you enjoy, but is it possible to change your routine to include more shared meals? Try not to miss this meaningful time with your family.

### 3. Establish Healthy Communication

Lastly, I'm sure you've heard the phrase "Communication is key." The breakdown of communication is often a major factor in broken relationships. You've probably also heard someone say that body language or nonverbals are 90 percent of how we communicate. That's a partial truth, because communication is actually 55 percent body language, 38 percent tone of voice, and 7 percent words spoken.[8] But this research brings me back to one of my previous points: When was the last time you had a conversation with your child while looking them directly in the eye (no distractions)?

I often talk to my kids when I'm making dinner, and while I'd like to think they enjoy this time with me, they and I know that they don't have my undivided attention. My daughter is often midsentence when I remember I forgot to grab a key ingredient at the store, and soon my mind is somewhere else. Even if I don't say it, she knows I'm distracted by my body language. That's why undistracted time should be a priority in building healthy communication with our kids.

Now, I don't want you to think you constantly have to drop whatever you're doing to process anything and everything with your kids. That's not sustainable, and you'll tire yourself out trying to do this. But I want you to start thinking about what you can do to limit distractions around dinnertime and bedtime—two of the best times to have those meaningful conversations.

**Practical Tips for Heart Connection**

- When your kids open up to you about difficult situations, don't jump into "fix-it mode" right away. Unsolicited advice is the number one conversation stopper. Take time to listen and reflect. It helps people feel heard.

- That being said, if your child is in danger or needs help, don't be afraid to share your wisdom and discernment with them.

- Pray and ask the Holy Spirit to guide your conversations and your tongue so you know if the situation warrants advice and intervention versus validation of feelings and a listening ear.

- Consider keeping a journal with your children in which you write back and forth to each other. Journals provide a space for children to ask questions or bring up topics they may be embarrassed to verbalize to you face-to-face.

As you focus on communicating with your family, you'll find what works and what doesn't. Trial and error may be a natural part of building communication. One last thought: don't be afraid to ask your child what helps them communicate best with you.

## Two Communication Techniques Counselors Use

To improve communication and build emotional depth in your family, here are two secret techniques counselors use all the time. I learned both in graduate school and use them when my kids need a little help exploring a hard-to-talk-about topic. Please don't try to use these two techniques in all your conversations. It's not necessary, and you will totally exhaust yourself. But if your child comes to you with a difficult problem or a heavy emotion, you'll have two wonderful tools at your disposal.

First, reflect their feeling. Young children may need assistance accurately articulating their complicated feelings. You can help by listening to them talk about the situation. Typically, you can identify their feeling for them by listening. Then you can share your insight by saying something like "That sounds really frustrating" or "If I were in that situation, I'd feel hurt." After listening to your child talk about the situation, restate the feeling. Then pause to give the child time to reflect further. By using this technique, not only will you help your child feel understood, but you'll also build their emotional awareness.

Second, summarize. It isn't uncommon for children to ramble or go on tangents when they're upset. You can help clearly define the problem and the situation by summarizing or restating back to them what you heard them say. Show your child you were actively listening and validate their feelings by bringing it all together in a brief summary.

If you need more details, questions like "Can you tell me more?" and "How did that make you feel?" could be helpful. Try to avoid asking "why" questions to get more information because they tend to put the person on the defensive and stop the conversation. Build the bridge of communication by actively listening to your child and reflecting back what you heard.

## Barriers to Winning Your Child's Heart

As we journey to intentionally win our children's hearts, some barriers may hold us back from nurturing them in the best ways possible. After talking with hundreds of parents over the past ten years, I've noticed three common parenting practices that limit our ability to build emotional connection and spiritual depth into our children's lives.

### 1. Parenting with Frustration

We've all had moments when we've lost our temper with our children. Parenthood is demanding and one of the most challenging jobs we will ever have. Kids push our buttons. It's natural to feel frustrated from time to time, but feeling frustrated with our kids shouldn't be a daily occurrence. Annoyance shouldn't be our first response. If this is true, we need to ask ourselves why this is happening.

It's common now for families to feel like they must do it all. I see parents putting way too much on their plates and instead of bringing abundance, it's bringing harm. When our schedules overwhelm us and we feel like we can never get anything done, we tend to take out our stress on the people around us. When we lose our temper with our children, we harm the connection we're trying to make with them. What happened to quality time together? To simpler lives? We sacrificed it in the name of providing a better future for our kids. We have to ask ourselves, Are all the extracurricular activities adding value to our lives or just more stress?

I'll never forget my daughter's piano teacher telling me, "Lauren, you'll be tempted to do all the activities, but you need to find a balance. Don't sacrifice family dinners and time together for extracurriculars. Everyone else may be doing it, but that doesn't mean you have to." I'm not saying we should never sign up for team sports or activities. Extracurriculars can be very enjoyable for everyone in the family, but when both parents work forty hours a week and run the kids to different places every night, it's no wonder they feel stressed and overwhelmed.

**Brain Builder:** We'll talk more about the importance of rest and how to create healthy family routines in chapter 11. For now, ask yourself, Do I struggle with parenting out of frustration? Do I believe the lie that I have to do it all, or is there another lie causing me to lose my temper with my family?

It's a vicious cycle. We strive to help our kids succeed in life, but the extra demands exhaust us. We end up taking it out on the ones we are trying to help. Then we feel guilty for yelling and blame ourselves for possibly harming our kids. We repeat the cycle, trying harder. Unfortunately, doing more doesn't always equal happier, healthier kids. In the rat race of parenting, we can't win.

This is one of those times when you need to ask God to search your heart and reveal the truth to you.

### 2. Parenting with Fear

This is a big one, and it may look different for each of us. After talking to hundreds of moms, I compiled a list of the most common fears modern parents experience. Take an honest look at the list below and ask yourself if you've ever feared your child will . . .

Be exposed to pornography, drugs, or twisted thinking, intentionally or unintentionally, taking away their innocence.

Be bullied, harassed, or made fun of by other children or even adults.

Be sexually molested.

Experience physical or emotional pain.

Lack knowledge of their true worth and believe the lie that they aren't special.

Struggle with sexual sin.

We naturally have a desire to protect and shield our children from the dangers of this world. That mama bear instinct is strong. The problem is when these fears turn into irrational beliefs and negatively impact how we parent. While I think it's wise to be cautious about the friends our children play with and the shows they watch on TV, overprotection based in fear causes more harm than good. If they see us making decisions out of fear, soon they will adopt this same framework too. Fearful parents raise fearful children.

119

As a parent, I know my children follow my lead, but sometimes when it comes to health stuff, it's hard for me to remain calm. This past winter we dealt with a lot of sicknesses, and my kids started to sense my unease. This was particularly true for two of my children. Every time their stomachs growled or grumbled, they panicked and thought they were about to get sick. It became a problem when it started to happen every night before bed, disrupting their sleep. In part, I believe the irrational fear manifested due to the unusual amount of sickness we had dealt with, but it was also caused by my fears related to health. We took it to God in prayer as a family and retrained our brains to feel peace even if our stomachs rumbled. With time, the irrational fears lessened, and sleep became sweet again. The fear may pop its head up again in the future, but now we know how to deal with it.

I'm sure all of us would agree that it's not good to walk around with fear every day. The trouble is, sometimes we don't think we have it. We mask our fear by calling it concern or wisdom or protection. I've heard people justify controlling their children's lives by saying, "I'm using wisdom." Though from an outside perspective, people can see that the control is at least partially rooted in fear. It's true, the Bible tells us to be sober-minded and alert. We must discern the times we live in and use wisdom to make decisions for our families, but our kids won't benefit from helicopter parenting or overprotection. Do we trust God will watch over them day and night or do we try to control the situation in our own strength? It's a delicate balance for sure. If this is something you struggle with, I want to challenge you to ask the Holy Spirit to bring to your awareness any lingering fear in your heart. If you have any irrational fears or beliefs, bring them to God. The Bible tells us in John 14:27,

> I am leaving you with a gift—peace of mind and heart. And the peace I give is a gift the world cannot give. So don't be troubled or afraid. (NLT)

We can't manufacture lasting peace in our own efforts. God gives us the gift of peace of mind and heart, but first, we must stop trying to get it in our own strength. Let God's Word wash over you. By doing this, you aren't only bringing inner peace to your spirit, but you're also showing your child we have a reason to hope. God is in control, and He loves you. Trust Him. Peace comes by trusting your Creator, not by controlling your surroundings.

### 3. Parenting without Discipline

When it comes to setting boundaries and healthy discipline, I like to think of the parent-child relationship as a bank account. As parents, at times we will make deposits into our children's accounts. For example, taking them out for ice cream, watching their favorite movie with them, or playing soccer with them in the backyard. Kids love deposits. But unfortunately, there will also be times when we need to withdraw from their accounts. Times when we have to say no, set a firm boundary, or discipline them for purposeful rebellion. That part isn't as much fun.

Recently I've noticed a shift in our culture. Parents seem to be making a lot more deposits than withdrawals. Have you noticed this too? For many parents, I think it's a reaction to their own childhood. The gravitation toward gentle parenting could be a result of the pain parents experienced in their childhood. There was a time when parents said things like "Stop crying or I'll give you something to cry about." Parents didn't think about emotional nourishment fifty, thirty, or even twenty years ago. Now it seems parenting is swinging in the other direction and parents are overemphasizing emotional well-being.

What does this have to do with our hearts? The more I've considered why parents are swinging in this direction and following gentle parenting, the more I believe it has to do with their heart posture. They could believe the lie that if their children feel pain because of them or if they somehow miss an emotional need, their children's hearts will become hardened or hurt beyond repair.

I understand people have been hurt by authoritarian parents or parents who were extremely demanding without any love or affection. That's not an ideal way to grow up. But a household without a balance of love and correction isn't good either.

From a biblical perspective, it's healthy to have a balance of *both* love and discipline. Correction doesn't need to be feared, and it doesn't need to be damaging. We can discipline without hardening our children's hearts.

Discipline isn't fun, but there's a reward, spiritual fruit, when you do it. Don't avoid making withdrawals because you fear discomfort.

 **Practical Discipline Tips**

Set firm and clear expectations for behavior in your family. Both parents should be on the same page when it comes to behavioral expectations. Can you define your limits, exceptions, and deal breakers? If not, I highly recommend having a conversation about it with your spouse.

Knowing the limits is so important, because when it comes to discipline, consistency is key. Kids thrive on consistency and knowing exactly what's expected when it comes to behavior. They become confused when the boundary lines keep changing, and it can cause even more outbursts.

Another strategy is to take emotion out of your discipline. When you yell and scream, your child tends to focus on your anger instead of their misbehavior. If that means you need to leave the room to calm down before you discipline, then do it.

Lastly, in the middle of a meltdown, be direct and succinct. Too much rambling causes kids to stop listening.

For the time being no discipline brings joy, but seems sad and painful; yet to those who have been trained by it, afterwards it yields the peaceful fruit of righteousness [right standing with God and a lifestyle and attitude that seeks conformity to God's will and purpose]. (Heb. 12:11 AMP)

Discipline is a healthy part of parenting. As much as I think it's essential for children to feel heard, we walk a fine line as parents. Validating kids' feelings and encouraging their hearts are huge parts of showing love, but love by itself won't raise an emotionally and spiritually healthy child. We also must factor in discipline and character building. It's healthy for us to challenge our kids in their weaknesses from time to time. That's where growth occurs.

It may not feel good when our kids are upset with us for setting a boundary or saying something they don't *want* to hear—even if they need to hear it. But God made us the authority figures in these relationships, so we must find that delicate balance. With practice and intention, we can parent successfully using both deposits of love and withdrawals of discipline.

## Final Thoughts on Emotional Connections and Discipline

Building heart connections at a young age establishes your relationship on a firm foundation. I truly believe that if we build emotional connections with our children when they're young, we set our relationships up for success when we walk with them through the storms of adolescence. Again, the trouble comes when we lean too hard on validating feelings and not enough on structure and discipline.

According to proponents of the gentle parenting perspective, parents should use emotional connection instead of punishment to raise happy and successful kids. On the one hand, I agree we should intentionally develop our children's emotional health and build beautiful connections with their hearts. We shouldn't provoke them to anger as the Bible tells us in Colossians 3:21. Nothing good comes from deliberately aggravating your child.

But on the other hand, gentle parenting puts too much emphasis on nurturing our children's feelings. Processing every single emotion we feel throughout the day isn't only exhausting, but it also teaches our children that our feelings have the final say. The problem is that feelings are fleeting, and we can't always trust them to be accurate. And unfortunately, our kids won't always feel happy, but that doesn't give them permission to melt down or give up.

Kids need to learn how to manage their big feelings, and they learn this through experience. Children shouldn't be prevented from experiencing negative emotions because we're afraid they might feel distress. Situations in which we feel uncomfortable are often where we learn grit, determination, and perseverance. We shouldn't prevent our children from experiencing these growth opportunities.

God is the perfect parent, and although His love for us is greater than we'll ever understand, He still allows us to walk through valleys. This doesn't mean we should constantly push our children to their limits or put them in unsafe situations, but we shouldn't fear negative emotions. God knows the seasons in which we struggle eventually lead to an abundant harvest. Give your kids the opportunity to grow instead of shielding them from all uncomfortable feelings.

Lastly, I believe many modern parenting practices leave out the parent's God-given role as the authority figure in a child's life. These days, parents are advised to let children negotiate limits and make their own choices to help them become more independent. I'd argue children don't need an equal say in discipline, and we need to stop giving our kids so many choices.

Kids can be thoughtless and make careless decisions without reason.

The Bible tells us, "Foolishness is bound up in the heart of a child; The rod of correction will drive it far from him" (Prov. 22:15). If you give a child a say in their punishment, more often than not they will try to avoid it. Not only that, but in life, we aren't able to negotiate everything.

Kids need to learn to follow directions and obey their superiors. When a parent says no, there should be no debate. And parents shouldn't have to overexplain why in order to parent with compassion. By honoring our parents, we respect their authority in our lives. Besides, when did obedience become a bad word? The Lord delights in obedience, as we see in 1 Samuel 15:22:

> But Samuel replied:
> "Does the LORD delight in burnt offerings and sacrifices
>     as much as in obeying the LORD?
> To obey is better than sacrifice,
>     and to heed is better than the fat of rams." (NIV)

Requiring obedience without offering choices or a chance to negotiate doesn't bring harm to our children's spirits. On the flip side, by offering choices all the time, parents unintentionally allow their children to become the authority figure in the relationship. I believe we, as Christian parents, are called to love, instruct, and guide our children. I'm not saying we have to be harsh or never give our kids choices. But kids shouldn't be given the heavy responsibility to make every decision about their life at such a young age. We should honestly ask ourselves the following questions: Are we allowing the kids to be the boss? Are we giving them the authority to determine their own boundaries and rules? God gave children parents for a reason. They need guidance and solid instruction. The best parents know how to balance grace and discipline.

## Best Practices for Parenting

I love when science catches up with the Bible. Psychology is now confirming that the best parenting practices use both love and structure. Researchers in human development have studied parenting styles for years. In 1971, Diana Baumrind gathered data on parenting styles by watching parents interact with their pre-schoolers. Her findings laid a foundation for child-rearing practices that experts still use today. She found four main parenting styles—authoritarian, authoritative, permissive, and uninvolved—and three main features—acceptance and involvement, control, and autonomy granting.

The most successful approach, authoritative, is warm and sensitive to a child's needs, places reasonable demands on the child, and encourages the child to make their own decisions when developmentally ready.[9] Authoritarian parents tend to demand a lot from their children, and they're not as warm and supportive, while indulgent or permissive parents are very loving and accepting without enforcing a lot of rules or control. Lastly, uninvolved parents are emotionally unavailable and place few demands or requests on the child.

Time and time again, research has shown that an authoritative parenting approach with a balance of both control and responsiveness is most beneficial for a child's social, intellectual, moral, and emotional growth. Children of authoritative parents tend to have healthier friendships, lower levels of risky behavior, and better overall emotional well-being.[10] Not only that, the supportive aspects of the authoritative approach, such as involvement and balanced control, are powerful sources of resilience in kids.[11] Isn't that what we want for our children? To learn how to handle adversity well? To live a life without torment or fear of obstacles?

As we close out the heart section of this book, I want you to remember this: discipline won't always be positive or fun, but it's a necessary part of parenting, and you don't have to dread it. Remind yourself what an honor and privilege it is to teach your children. To instruct and shape their tiny hearts, which God entrusted to us. You can't do it alone, but you have the ultimate Helper at your side. He'll show you the perfect combination of endless love and corrective instruction.

# 8

# Our Identity as Children of God

One humid summer night, I almost gave up the fight. Cars, building blocks, diapers, ABC worksheets, and coloring pencils cluttered the living room floor. As I let out a scream after stepping on a LEGO piece, I remembered I had forgotten to move the laundry from the washer to the dryer the night before. I was exhausted and tired of cleaning up after everyone. But the mess in the house felt like the least of my problems.

My mind raced as we tucked our three children in for the night. The goal was to get our kids to bed as fast as possible because I needed to talk to my husband about what I'd seen that day. Our bedtime routine seemed to drag on longer than usual, but finally we had only one more kid to tuck in. I felt my chest tighten as I sang her to sleep, "God's got a plan for your life, and He'll always be there." I sing those words to our children every night, but that night the words took on a deeper meaning. I heard a small, still voice ask me, "Do you really believe the words you're singing? Lauren, do you trust Me with your children's lives?"

God challenged my anxious heart, but I felt too emotionally drained to respond to His probing questions.

As soon as the kids fell asleep, I collapsed onto our bed, putting my body at ease for the first time all day. Our three active kids find an incredible amount of joy in jumping, running, and screaming around the house each day. It isn't easy to find peace and silence, but the house finally seemed quiet. The only problem was that my heart couldn't find the words to speak.

Earlier in the day, I'd received numerous messages from friends and acquaintances who wanted to know what I thought about the latest news. They asked, "Aren't you afraid for your children?" and "What will you tell your kids?" Their questions came from a place of love. They knew we were raising biracial children, and they were curious. But their innocent questions seemed to confirm in my already troubled heart that I should indeed be worried.

As I stared at the ceiling fan in our bedroom, I struggled to find the words to speak to my husband. I could never unsee the video I'd watched of the murder of George Floyd. The images I saw and the questions I heard kept replaying in my mind.

With a million thoughts in my head, I looked over at my sweet husband, who happens to be African American, and asked, "What do you think about all this? Should we be concerned?"

When my husband is conflicted, he usually retreats and remains quiet. His hesitation in answering my question revealed to me that he was deep in thought. After letting out a slow exhale, he said in his calm, steady voice, "Lauren, this isn't good. But we aren't going to worry about our kids. And we aren't going to tell our kids life is always going to be hard for them because of the color of their skin. What does God say about who we are?" My mind went back to the prompting I'd heard earlier from God. Did I trust God with my children? Did I believe His promises for my family?

"I know. You're right. But life seems so heavy right now, and everything I hear on the news makes me feel like I'm supposed to be afraid," I said.

The world was seemingly falling to pieces. We'd been in quarantine for months because of the COVID-19 pandemic, and every day as I poured my coffee into my "Strong as a Mother" mug, I felt like a fraud. "Stressed as a Mother" seemed to better describe my attitude. I was on Mom Duty 24/7. Self-care had flown out the window and hadn't even said goodbye. And my soul longed for a break from the chaos surrounding me. I knew I had to be strong for my family, but I didn't know how.

After several moments of silence, my husband continued, "The world may tell us one thing, but God has the final say over our identity. All authority belongs to Him."

Our conversation stopped my mental spiral and stirred my spirit. We'd always taken our roles as parents seriously. For years my heart longed to raise healthy, godly children who did more than just survive in life, but we'd never faced such a broken world before. Life's obstacles put our parenting to the test. Were we preparing our kids to go out into the real world? How could we help them thrive even amid darkness?

Our children were looking to *us* for wisdom, understanding, direction, and comfort. That night we wrestled with the concerns of the world and the truth of God's Word. The world told us, "Your children are in danger because of the color of their skin. They'll always have to work harder and smarter." But my husband reminded me that God speaks a better word. As children of God, we are complete in Him (Col. 2:10), and oppression is far from us. Therefore, we don't have to fear (Isa. 54:14).

Life will throw us curveballs, some strong enough to knock us down. But at the end of the day, we decide what we want to pay attention to and what voice we want to believe. The final word on our lives belongs to God, not culture. The trouble is, having no idea who God says we are leaves us vulnerable to believing the lies the world tells us. Seeds of identity are planted early in a child's life and growing them is a worthy endeavor. Kids who have a solid foundation of faith are better able to face the dark, scary world without losing their faith or integrity. Intentionally build your child's identity in Jesus. When children know who they are, they're less likely to give in to temptation or become discouraged by life's obstacles.

But like many areas in this book, it starts with us, the parents. Who are we? Whose voice are we listening to about our worth? The answers to those questions will determine what seeds we plant in our children's lives. Uncertain parents can't raise confident kids. For kids to develop a strong identity in Christ, parents need to understand their own identity first.

## Who God Says I Am

Only one voice has the final say, and that's the God of the universe. So, what does He say about us?

If you've never intentionally studied what Scripture says about your God-given identity, I highly recommend it. In appendix B, you'll find a list of twenty verses related to identity to help you get started. Memorize the truth, because the enemy will whisper

**Faith Former:** Pause and study the Scripture verses below.

We were created to do good works (Eph. 2:10).

We are loved deeply by the creator of the heavens and the earth (Eph. 3:18; John 3:16).

We were created with intention (Ps. 139:16) and in God's image (Gen. 1:27).

We are victorious (1 John 4:4) and filled with power, love, and a sound mind (2 Tim. 1:7).

We are blessed with every spiritual blessing because we sit with Christ in the heavenly realms right now (Eph. 1:3; 2:6).

partial truths into your ear. And the lies may not seem like lies at first because they contain an ounce of truth. The devil is a deceiver and a distracter. He doesn't play fair. You must know the truth to have a solid rebuttal to his accusations. Jesus resisted the devil in the desert by knowing the truth of God's Word. When the devil twisted God's Word and tempted Jesus, Jesus always responded with "It is written . . ." He didn't worship or pray the enemy away; He firmly and confidently spoke the truth of God's Word. You and your children must do the same.

## Jesus Loves Me

A few years ago, I listened to a testimony at church and the man said something I'll never forget. He said, "I never doubted God existed. I always believed Jesus came to this earth and that He is God's only Son. The problem wasn't that I didn't believe in God. I didn't believe He could love someone as broken as me." As I listened to the man speak, tears formed in my eyes. Because I needed that reminder. I've walked with God most of my life, but I'd be lying if I said there were never days or seasons when my heart questioned if God truly cared for me. Why is it that when we're waiting for a breakthrough or an answer to prayer, that's when the enemy whispers in our ears? He says, "If God really loved you, this wouldn't be happening" or "Well, you're not getting the answer to your prayer because God doesn't really care about you."

This is what the enemy does. He makes us question God's love for us. His lies drive us to doubt who God created us to be. And if we spend all our time questioning who we are and whether God *really* loves us, then we miss out on the purposes He has set before us. However, when we know exactly who we are as children of God, we walk in the power and authority He's given us. We don't waste time questioning if God treasures us; our hearts know it deeply. His hidden Word in our hearts shields us from the lies of the enemy. What a difference our identity makes in our lives. Imagine a generation where every individual knew exactly who they were created to be.

## How to Teach Our Children Their True Worth

You may be beginning to see how closely interconnected our minds, hearts, and identities are. While we've moved on to shaping our children's identities and building their faith, you'll notice this chapter also includes tools and strategies to build our children's overall emotional well-being. As I studied faith formation and how to cultivate a biblical identity within our children, I found seven areas to focus on: memorizing Scripture, worshiping as a family, learning how to pray, living with bold faith, growing in community, discipling intentionally, finding God in everyday life.

I've said it before, but I'll say it again—this list wasn't created to make you feel like you need to do all the things all day, every day. The goal is to take an honest look at the areas you do well in and the areas in which you can improve. If you need to make changes in your parenting, don't overwhelm yourself or your family by trying to do it all at once. Start slowly, and intentionally choose one area to work on each month.

### 1. Memorizing Scripture

In kindergarten, our oldest daughter's class memorized Psalm 23. As a result of her practicing each night, our family ended up memorizing it together. Scripture is a weapon. It's one of the best ways to fight back against the enemy's lies. For our kids to know their authority as children of God, we need to teach them His Word. Hide God's Word in your heart, and when you need refreshment, the Holy Spirit will remind you of it at the perfect time (John 14:26). This is true for adults and children. A few months after memorizing Psalm 23, our youngest child had a medical emergency. Our world was in the middle of a pandemic, and the last place we wanted to end up was in the emergency room with our baby.

We tried to remain calm, but our children sensed our anxiety. Our oldest daughter, without prompting, folded her hands and started praying Psalm 23. In the middle of this tense situation, I almost burst into tears as she prayed a powerful prayer over her sister. Thankfully, with medication and prayer, we didn't end up in the emergency room. That night as I went to bed, I thanked God for bringing His Word back to our daughter's mind.

When we memorize Scripture, we have a weapon to fight against fear, anxiety, lies, and overwhelm. Even children as young as two or three can start memorizing Scripture. Help them hide as much of it as possible in their hearts so that when the tough times come, they have a weapon waiting to help them battle through.

### 2. Worshiping as a Family

Last Sunday, I helped in the elementary room at church, and when it was time for worship, the kids stood and sang but remained as stiff as boards through all the songs. The mood in the room felt so serious. Now, I know everyone has their personal preferences when it comes to worship, but I'd seen these kids dance and run and sing before. Only it was to secular music like "The Gummy Bear Song" and "Can't Stop the Feeling!" from the movie *Trolls*. While I think it's important for kids to have a reverence for all things holy, when kids view church as strict and serious, they don't feel 100 percent comfortable opening up to God. In the Bible, we see David, a grown man, dancing before the Lord with all his might (2 Sam. 6:14).

Worship shouldn't be mechanical; it should be an honest, heartfelt expression of our admiration for God. Yes, we need to be careful we don't get off track, and we should worship according to biblical instruction. But praising God should also be fun. We can help our children see this by playing praise and worship music when we're in the car, making dinner, or running around outside. Plan a family worship night once a week or once a month. Sing praises to God together as a family. Give the Holy Spirit a chance to speak and move in your midst. Rote worship isn't impactful and leads to dead religion. Allow the joyful spirit God has placed in your heart to shine. Worshiping as a family in spirit and truth will leave a lasting imprint on your child's heart.

### 3. Learning How to Pray

It wasn't until I was in my midtwenties that I became comfortable with praying out loud. I prayed in my head a lot, but if someone was needed to pray aloud at youth group or church, I'd never volunteer. While I think it's okay to recite Scripture or speak words of encouragement in our minds, there's power when we pray out loud. Spoken prayer shows our spirits, God, and the devil that we mean business. If you've never prayed out loud before, it's normal to feel a bit hesitant. There is no "right" way to pray; God simply wants to talk and commune with you. If you or your child feel nervous about praying out loud, start with a small phrase. Prayer doesn't have to be perfect. Start somewhere, and with time and practice, you and your kids will gain confidence.

Ideally, you'll want to start teaching your kids to pray when they're young and less self-conscious. Pray together as a family and include your toddler in prayer time. They can say, "Thank You, Jesus" and "Amen." Start with something as simple as that. Soon prayer will become second nature to them.

Prayer should be a part of your daily life, and your kids should hear you communicate with God too. Pray in front of them. Obviously, if you don't think certain topics are appropriate for little ears to hear, pray those prayers in private. But ultimately, you want to expose your children to prayer frequently and find opportunities for them to see the power of prayer manifest.

## 4. Living with Bold Faith

For the most part, our kids get along well together. But as with any family, there are days when they purposefully annoy each other. Last summer there were too many days when sibling frustration led to an exchange of angry words. Our children needed to learn the importance of the tongue and its impact on those around them.

A few weeks after talking at dinner about the power of the tongue, our family had a practical application moment. Our two-year-old hit her top front tooth hard on our small trampoline, and within a few days, the tooth turned completely gray. Thankfully it was a baby tooth and there was no significant damage, but the dentist told me her tooth would most likely stay fully gray until it fell out years later. The tooth didn't cause her any pain, and it wasn't a huge deal, but I felt a twinge of sadness every time her big, beautiful smile showed a dark tooth. I told our older kids, "You know what? This is a chance to speak life over your sister's tooth. The power of life and death is in your tongue!" So, every day for a week we told her tooth to live and not die. We took turns praying over it and believing God's Word.

One morning as I was changing my daughter's diaper, I screamed. My entire family immediately came running. My son asked, "What's wrong, Mom?" I said, "Look! Doesn't it look like her tooth is whiter?" I quickly took a photo and compared it to a picture I had taken the week before. Sure enough, it looked lighter. Within a few days, her tooth turned completely white again. After a quick online search, I learned baby teeth can turn back to their normal color after trauma, but it takes a long time—at least six months.[1] We saw it happen in less than two weeks. I believe God heard our prayers and honored the life-giving words coming out of our mouths. As parents, we should look for moments like this because they give our kids a real-life experience with God. Having knowledge of the Bible is important, but experiences where kids see that God is real are what strengthen their faith.

### 5. Growing in Community

God created us to be in relationships with one another. Friends who sharpen and encourage us make walking this faith journey a little bit easier and a whole lot less lonely. As we learned earlier, we are all influenced by the people we interact with on a regular basis. If we want to build emotional and spiritual depth in our children, we need to help them find life-giving friendships. We often tell them they don't need a ton of friends. Sometimes one or two friends who we can trust completely is better than ten friends who influence us negatively. As parents, we should encourage our children to connect with friends who will be positive influences in their lives.

Because we are called to be set apart from this world, friendship can sometimes be difficult. Children may be tempted to fit in and sacrifice their morals for the sake of friendship. This is why it's important to find relationships in faith-filled communities. There's a higher chance your kids will find friends who sharpen instead of hinder their walk with God. We all need to find a place where we belong. If kids have a solid group of like-minded friends with whom they can bond and gather, the pressure to conform won't feel as constricting. If you aren't involved in a church with an active children's ministry or youth group, I highly recommend you talk to your pastor about starting one or look for a church with a thriving children's ministry. We need one another, and faith-filled friendships are extremely valuable to building strong spiritual and emotional health.

### 6. Discipling Intentionally

Finding a healthy church community to be a part of is a beautiful way to engage in and build up the body of Christ. But we can't rely solely on someone else to add spiritual depth to our children's lives. Discipling intentionally is one of the key aspects of laying a firm foundation of faith over time.

What is discipling? It's the deliberate act of teaching and instructing someone in the ways of God. Kids need guidance early on in their faith walks. Parents can provide this instruction by reading the Bible with their children and helping kids apply biblical principles to their everyday lives. Many of the Faith Former activities you've learned in this book can help you disciple intentionally.

The other day I went to breakfast with the wife of our church's youth pastor. We started talking about college, and I asked her, "What makes the difference between a child who goes off to college and walks away from his faith and the one who goes off and instead grows in his faith?" She thought for a moment, then told me that, in her experience, when she saw kids studying the Bible and seeking Jesus on their own time, they were more likely to stay strong in their faith. While a person can certainly learn these behaviors themselves, parents have a unique opportunity to disciple their children and teach them how to study God's Word at a young age so one day in the future they are able to study it on their own.

Remember, your instruction doesn't need to be formal. I often go on tangents with my children as topics come up. The other day our eight-year-old daughter asked what a bikini was because some of her friends at school said they'd be wearing one at the end-of-year pool party. I used her question as a learning opportunity. In addition to discussing swimsuits and why we shouldn't show too much skin, we looked up Scripture verses on modesty. Thankfully we'd recently bought a faith-based girl's book on maturing bodies, *The Ultimate Girls' Body Book*, and it had a section on dressing modestly. Conversations about biblical principles occur over time. Discipleship is not a once-and-done process.

### 7. Finding God in Everyday Life

Lastly, to give our children opportunities to truly experience the goodness of God at a young age, we must keep our eyes open. God is all around, but often we are too busy to see Him. Find opportunities to pray, serve, and love your neighbor.

I understand tasks take longer when you invite children into them. Sometimes I'd rather make dinner myself because it's faster, less messy, and more efficient. But kids miss out on practical teaching moments when we leave them out of the process. If we want our children to know God, we should give them opportunities to meet Him.

Obviously praying before bed is a great first step. Reading the Bible together as a family is another. But one of the best things you can do is lead by example. Our children watch us, and as a result, they learn through observation. If they see Mom and Dad praying together every morning, they know prayer is important. Not because you told them it is, but because they saw you walk it out. Day and night, you can tell your kids that God should be number one in their lives, but if they don't see you putting God first, your words mean nothing. While instructing our children is a huge part of building their faith, modeling a healthy relationship with God brings it all together. Parents build their children's faith by what they teach and what they model.

**Faith Former:** Brainstorm ways you can bring God into your family's everyday life. For example, when you drive by an accident, pray out loud for the families involved. Take turns praying before dinner. We even give our two-year-old a turn in the rotation. If you make a meal to take to another family in need, get your kids involved. They can design a card or help prepare the food.

## Lessons from Daniel

Intentional parenting matters. We see a few examples of it in the Bible, one of my favorites being in the book of Daniel. Here we see teenagers who held on to their God-given identities and a clear picture of how an identity rooted in Christ changes a life.

While today's culture might seem more evil than ever before, it's not the first time godly people have had to live in a corrupt society. Daniel and his friends became separated from their families and taken captive by the Babylonians in 605 BC when they were only teenagers. They were alienated from their families, churches, and homeland. Their entire lives were turned upside down. Because Daniel and his friends were handsome and intelligent, they were appointed to work in the king's palace (Dan. 1:4). Daniel was given the name Belteshazzar, and his friends were called Meshach, Shadrach, and Abed-Nego.

As part of their training, the palace served the teens the king's delicacies to eat, but Daniel purposed in his heart that he would not defile himself with food and drink dedicated to false gods (v. 8). Instead of the king's food, Daniel asked if he and his friends could eat vegetables and drink water instead. The steward overseeing their training agreed to Daniel's request. Even when everyone around him followed the king's orders, Daniel refused to give in to something he knew in his heart was wrong.

It's important to note that Daniel's parents weren't around to guide him in this decision. No one suggested he do this; he felt it in his heart. How did that happen? I believe Daniel's parents did an excellent job of instilling godly wisdom in him at a young age so that it stayed with him even when he was separated from them. Daniel walked out the faith he gained as a young child. This is the first example we see in the book of Daniel where young men went against the culture to stand for something they believed in. God honored Daniel's faithfulness, and he and his friends continued to grow in wisdom, knowledge, understanding, and health (vv. 15, 17).

Later we read that King Nebuchadnezzar constructed and worshiped an image of gold. He instructed everyone in the kingdom to worship the gold image, and if they failed to do so, they'd be thrown immediately into a burning fiery furnace (Dan. 3:4–6). The friends' faithfulness to God was tested again. Would they give in to the corrupt moral climate surrounding them? Would they do something against their faith to avoid punishment? It's impressive to think that teenagers who'd been separated from their entire lives and put in a completely new environment stood up to a threatening king. I believe their courage came from knowing exactly who they were in God. They also knew the God of the universe would make a way to save them from the fiery furnace and the king's anger. After the king threw Shadrach, Meshach, and Abed-Nego into the furnace, we read in Daniel 3:24–25,

> Then King Nebuchadnezzar was astonished; and he rose in haste and spoke, saying to his counselors, "Did we not cast three men bound into the midst of the fire?" They answered and said to the king, "True, O king." "Look!" he answered, "I see four men loose, walking in the midst of the fire; and they are not hurt, and the form of the fourth is like the Son of God."

God came through. Just like they did for Daniel, tough times will come for our children, so we must teach them to walk with integrity even if it's scary. Because of their solid identity in God, the young men were able to stand up against the evils of the culture in which they lived, and their faith even turned a king's heart. Daniel and his friends weren't influenced by the culture in which they lived; instead, their actions changed the culture. I love how pastor Matt Webel puts it:

> Taken captive by a hostile culture, Daniel didn't wither or give in, but flourished and transformed it! Daniel's bold faithfulness

resulted in kings being converted, kingdoms being overturned, and even Christ being worshipped by the Magi centuries later.[2]

This is why intentional parenting matters. Knowing who you are helps you find your true purpose and stay focused on the tasks God puts before you. Like Daniel and his friends, your children can be firmly planted in their convictions and not be swayed by popular culture. Right now, you're laying the foundation that will shape not only your children's futures but possibly that of an entire generation.

# 9

# Building Your Child's Self-Esteem

One day last week, I walked into our dining room and saw our youngest child sitting under the table with a pair of blunt-tip scissors. Whether she chose that spot to hide from me or to take advantage of the warm sunlight shining through the window, I'll never know. Either way, she had no idea how to use scissors. At least I'd never taken the time to show her how to cut correctly. But in typical third-child fashion, she confidently told herself, "I can do it all by myself. I just put my finger in here and cut."

Before I intervened, I observed her for a bit. She had a fierce look of determination as she cut that piece of construction paper into the smallest pieces she could. One minute she'd say, "I can do it" and smile from ear to ear. The next, she'd shout in frustration, "Mommy, I can't do it. I need help!" While she had high expectations for herself, realistically her cutting skills weren't great, and it made her very mad.

Many of us have experienced this same type of frustration when our intentions didn't match our abilities. We may even feel that tension when it comes to parenting. We desire to raise unshakable kids who excel in life, but too many times we doubt and cry out, "I need help!" We wrestle with feelings of anxiety, frustration, and worry. No one likes to sit in that tension.

The ability to take the next step and find breakthrough when the going gets tough is what makes the difference between people who stay stuck and those who flourish. You took that first step by picking up this book. Now, in this chapter, you'll learn how to help your kids push on and have confidence in themselves to do the hard things. It starts with having good, healthy self-esteem. Because self-esteem is a large part of emotional well-being, we'll explore how to help kids build and maintain it, so when they experience challenges, mistakes, or frustration, they don't lose all hope.

## What Is Self-Esteem?

Let's start by looking at what self-esteem is exactly. The department of sociology at the University of Maryland defines self-esteem this way: "Self-esteem is a positive or negative orientation toward oneself; an overall evaluation of one's worth or value."[1] In other words, self-esteem is characterized by how someone views themselves and the value they place on themselves.

Most developmental psychologists agree that self-esteem is important, and they've found it develops quite early. By the age of four, children have formed several self-judgments; for example, they can tell you how well they learn things in school, their ability to make friends, and how well they get along with their parents.[2] Young children pay attention to social behavior and compare themselves to others. By the age of five, children develop a sense of self-esteem comparable in strength to that of an adult.[3]

As you can see, children make conclusions about their abilities early on, which impacts their self-esteem moving forward. It makes sense why parents would want to learn how to build healthy self-esteem in their kids at a young age.

## How to Build Healthy Self-Esteem

What's one of the best ways to build healthy self-esteem in children? Build a healthy identity first. Identity and self-esteem are closely related. While identity is knowing who we are, self-esteem is having confidence in who God created us to be. A person with high self-esteem recognizes and values their God-given talents, gifts, and abilities. We spent an entire chapter looking at our biblical identity and finding ways to build a foundation of faith in our children.

When our children's identities don't originate with God, they derive their self-worth from the world. Unfortunately, the world's version of identity contradicts most of what the Bible says. The world tells us we can do anything we want and our strength comes from ourselves, but we know that without God, all things are *not* possible. Our Creator *has* to be part of the picture, because He designed it all with intention. When we put our confidence in our own strengths and abilities, it's almost a guarantee that we'll be disappointed. The people and things of this world will fail us at one point or another. Then what happens to our identity and self-worth? They crumble.

When we pause and think about it, putting our hope in worldly things limits us from finding lasting stability, comfort, and peace. Over the last decade, there has been an overall increase in anxiety in the United States,[4] and one possible reason for this is that we have put our hope in corruptible things. Then when life gets bumpy, we don't have solid hope to stand on. But when we have a strong foundation and put our trust and hope in the Lord, we will be blessed (Jer. 17:7). The *Full Life Study Bible* explains this biblical truth well:

> Those whose trust centers in themselves and in human resources are destined for disappointment, spiritual poverty, and ultimate loss. On the contrary, those who fully trust in the Lord will be blessed and ultimately rewarded with a godly inheritance. They will not fear or be anxious in any of life's circumstances because their roots go down deep into God.[5]

In times of adversity, when by all accounts we should be stressed, we can stand in peace. Why? Because our identities are deeply rooted in Christ. And when we put our trust in the Lord, with God's help, we find the grit, endurance, and confidence to keep pushing forward no matter the circumstance. Though it seems counter to what the world says, our evaluation of our worth must include God.

In this chapter, you'll learn research-backed psychological tools to help build healthy self-esteem in your child. But remember this: the strongest self-esteem is rooted in Christ.

## Taking a Self-Esteem Temperature Check

Now that we know exactly what self-esteem is, let's see how our self-esteem is doing. One of the best ways to take a temperature check on our self-esteem is by listening to our self-talk. Self-talk is what we say to ourselves in our heads or what we say out loud about ourselves. It can be negative or positive. Whether or not we realize it, our inner dialogue never ends. We constantly make quick judgments throughout the day and either encourage or discourage ourselves with our self-talk.

As you can imagine, if we constantly say negative things about ourselves or to ourselves, we won't build up our self-esteem. However, self-talk filled with life and encouragement causes our self-worth to naturally rise. There's been a great deal of research conducted on self-talk and self-esteem. A notable study with kids found that positive self-talk was positively related to self-esteem and negatively related to irrational beliefs and depression.[6] So not only will positive self-talk boost our self-esteem, it may be a protective factor against depression and irrational beliefs.

Sounds easy enough, right? The hard part for many of us, kids and adults included, is we may not even realize the things we say to ourselves until we stop and think about them. As you

**Brain Builder:** Take an inventory of your self-talk. If your child is old enough, they can participate in this activity as well. If you have a younger child, you can do it for them. Listen and take inventory of what you say throughout the day. How do you respond when you are playing or working and come across a challenge?

Ask yourself (or your child):

Do my thoughts encourage me throughout the day? Or do they bring more self-doubt?
How often do I complain to myself?
Am I quick to criticize myself when I do something wrong?
When I face a challenge, what's the first thing I say?

If you find that most of your commentary is negative or critical, you may have low self-esteem. If your commentary is split, you have average self-esteem.

gain metacognition—the ability to think about your thinking—you can identify if your self-talk is mostly negative or positive.

Don't panic if you or your child's self-talk or self-esteem isn't where you'd like it to be. Whether or not you realized it, you started to change both of them in the mind chapters by challenging the negative beliefs you held about yourself. You continued this work by completing the Brain Builders. If you or your child struggle in the area of self-esteem, remember that it can be transformed! It may take time to develop and change, so give yourself grace in the process.

## Model Positive Self-Talk

Need a self-talk boost? Here's a simple thing you can do to improve your child's self-talk: model positive self-talk throughout the day. It may seem silly at first, but it's great for kids to hear your thought process. Many pediatricians encourage parents to verbalize what they're doing throughout the day, even if their babies can't respond, because it's great for language development. Take the talking a step further and reveal your feelings as you speak. Then you're not only helping your child's language development, but you're also supporting their emotional development.

You can share how you overcame something hard at the dinner table or in the middle of the situation. I often model self-talk by saying something like "I am feeling flustered. I have so much to do! Breathe, Lauren. It'll be okay. Just take one step at a time. With a little bit of work, you can get everything done." Kids benefit from hearing our problem-solving strategies and expression of feelings. As you know, children are always listening, so modeling positive self-talk is a great way to influence their emotional intelligence indirectly.

## Take It a Step Further

If your child is struggling to improve their self-talk on their own, there's something you can do as the parent to encourage it. However, it may not be what you think. Our first instinct may be to offer more praise and encouragement. Hold that thought for a moment, we'll get there soon. Unfortunately, praise alone won't do it. Instead of offering more encouragement, ask questions.

It's better for compliments to come from ourselves rather than our peers. While it's nice to be praised and applauded, the most powerful praise comes from our own lips. When a child says, "I'm brave," they're more likely to believe it than when an adult tells them, "You are so brave." Praise is good from parents, but it's even better when kids say positive things about themselves.

Questions like these get kids to think about how they were able to do something hard. Not only will their responses get them to speak positively about themselves, but the thoughtful questions will also help them identify coping strategies that work for them.

**Brain Builder:** Ask your child these targeted questions to build their self-esteem and get them talking about themselves! While this list of questions is a great start to get your kids praising themselves, feel free to add your own questions.

How did you pull off that difficult task?

I know a lot of kids who would have given up by now. How did you manage to keep going?

I would've been so mad if that had happened to me. How did you stay calm?

At first, you were very frustrated, but then you stuck with it and did it. How did you keep going even when it was hard?

I know you were really disappointed you couldn't (fill in the blank). How did you make yourself feel better?"

## The Right Kind of Praise

Okay, now it's time to talk about praise. Have you ever heard someone say, "Don't praise your kids"? People who advocate limited praise also say you shouldn't tell your kids "good job." I've heard variations of this advice over the years, and it's time we get some clarity on it. Never encouraging our kids seems harsh and unrealistic. We'll make ourselves go crazy by constantly thinking about what we should and shouldn't say. "Ah, I just told my child good job. He's ruined for life!"

Seems a bit dramatic, right? Is "good job" the best type of praise we can give our children? Probably not. It's not specific and feels a bit superficial. But should we spend hours worrying about how many times we told our children "good job" or "you're so pretty" when they were young and whether we ruined their self-esteem because of it? Definitely not. Their self-esteem is not *that* fragile. However, some praise seems to be better than others.

Researchers at Columbia University found that children who were praised for their intelligence cared more about their performance than children who were praised for their effort.[7] What does this mean? One could interpret the results and conclude that when parents tell their children a variation of "you are so smart," the statement unintentionally causes the child to become hyperfocused on task performance.

As a result, when a child fixates on performance and intelligence, they can start to think, *If I fail, then I'm not smart anymore* . . . See how this could be a problem? The researchers also found that when children who were praised for their intelligence failed at the task, they were less likely to persist, had lower task enjoyment, and performed worse overall than children who were praised for their effort.[8] Because of this research, many people conclude that certain types of praise are better than others.

It makes sense that a child praised for their effort will persist in the task longer. You should encourage your kids to keep trying when the going gets tough. Praise them in the process. You'll never go wrong by developing skills like grit, persistence, and endurance in your kids.

Process praise is always good, but does that mean all types of praise are beneficial? Some experts argue parents should never comment on things children have no control over, such as intelligence, physical attractiveness, and athletic ability. However, I believe it's natural for parents to want to encourage and praise their kids for these things. I believe it's the way God designed us. Have my husband and I told our children they're smart? Yes, we have. I believe we should celebrate the fact that God has given all of us a brain and the ability to learn. Have we also told our children they look beautiful? Yes.

The other day I watched as my husband walked down the stairs and greeted our youngest daughter. She'd just put on her new dress, and as soon as she saw my husband, she started twirling. With an enormous smile on her face, she said, "Look,

Daddy!" Even at a young age, she wanted him to notice her beauty. She wanted him to comment on her new dress. I continued watching as my husband said, "Wow, you look so beautiful," and our daughter's smile got even bigger. Her face lit up because of his compliment. To me, eliminating this type of praise is a bit extreme.

While scientific research is valuable and can give us tools to better develop our children, it's not the be-all and end-all. I have a hard time believing that occasionally praising things like intelligence, physical attractiveness, and athletic ability is highly detrimental to a child's development. Yes, I can see where it could become problematic if a child hears this type of praise all day, every day, but praise and encouragement are natural parts of the parent-child relationship. There needs to be a balance between praising your kids for their effort and praising them for their unique gifts, talents, and abilities; don't go to extremes in either direction. God knows our hearts better than any researcher could ever begin to understand. Consider the science, then ask God to bring the right words to your lips when talking to your kids, and He will do it. Pray and trust God will show you the way.

Lastly, I don't want you to read this section and become so hypersensitive about the right praise that you miss out on those precious moments to connect heart to heart with your kids.

## Too Much Praise and Encouragement?

Now that we've analyzed the types of praise, let's look at the amount of praise a child should receive. Is there such a thing as too much praise? According to research, the answer is yes, too much praise can be detrimental instead of beneficial to a child's self-esteem. Developmental psychologist Dr. Eddie Brummelman found that adults are more likely to give personal praise (e.g., "You're smart!") and inflated praise (e.g., "That's incredibly beautiful!") to children with low self-esteem, which causes their feelings of self-worth to decrease instead of increase.[9] That isn't what you'd expect, right? Shouldn't more praise and encouragement boost a child's self-esteem?

Kids can sense when adults try to lavish them with over-the-top amounts of praise. Too much praise can make the words feel insincere. Children realize when the comments are untrue, and this can lead them to question why an adult is telling them that their mediocre drawing is spectacular. While praise is a form of encouragement and can be used to inspire our children, we need to be careful not to overdo it.

## The Pressure to Perform

Along with keeping our praise at appropriate levels, we want to make sure we don't offer praise only when our children excel. I've seen well-meaning parents put unintentional pressure on their children to perform by only praising their successes. We should encourage our children to succeed or fail no matter what. Praise isn't inherently wrong, but we don't want it to get into a pattern where our kids think they'll only receive recognition from us if they achieve something.

Watching our children be the best in arts or sports can be thrilling. As parents, it's natural to have hopes and dreams for them. We desire for our children to have better lives than we did, and we want them to reach their full potential. So when our children win a medal in swimming or get first place in an art competition, of course we want to praise them. Celebrating our children's wins is important, but we need to be careful not to put unnecessary pressure on them to succeed in order to earn praise. Praise from our lips shouldn't come only when they win. A parent's love, attention, devotion, and encouragement shouldn't be solely linked to performance.

Kids strive to impress their parents, and that's okay, but it's dangerous when kids believe they'll only be appreciated or praised if they "perform." Then they'll feel pressured to continually do so. Our support and encouragement shouldn't be conditional. A parent's love should be available to a child at all times. Words of encouragement shouldn't come from our mouths only when our kids hit a home run or score 100 percent on a math test. To avoid the pressure to perform, we need to remind our children often that our love for them never changes even if they fail.

## How to Handle Mistakes

This idea that our love for our children never changes even if they fail brings us to how to handle mistakes. Starting at a young age, children can feel pressure to always get everything right. They might want to avoid mistakes to please their parents or satisfy an innate desire to succeed. To make matters worse, young children often have a low frustration tolerance. Has your child ever cried or gotten upset because his drawing didn't "look right"? Has your daughter ever thrown a tantrum because her tower kept falling over when she tried to add another block? It's normal for young kids to feel big emotions about mistakes or deemed failures. Our children should know that we still love them and believe in them during these times, but it goes beyond showing them love. We also want to show them how to confront or move past their real or perceived weaknesses.

To do this, kids need to learn they'll make mistakes. No one is perfect. Mistakes are a part of life. Our drawings won't always be flawless, our towers won't always be unbreakable, and our cartwheels won't always be perfect. At some point, our children need to confront the fact that they'll fail. As parents, we can encourage them in the process.

We can use process praise, which means acknowledging a child's effort instead of the outcome. Your child may be painting a rainbow, but all the colors are mixing and it's difficult to tell it's a rainbow. Instead of saying it's beautiful when both you and your child know it's not, you could point out how hard they worked on the piece of art. "Wow, I love how you tried really hard to use all the colors and you didn't give up. You kept painting even when it wasn't turning out exactly how you imagined." You don't have to say it's good when it's not, but you can praise their effort.

We want our children to learn to persevere. People build endurance and grit by making mistakes, being uncomfortable, and pushing through. We must give our kids the opportunity to keep trying even if it's hard. Don't back away from a task because your child might have a meltdown if they don't get it just "right." Teach them tools like taking a few deep breaths or engaging in positive self-talk to push past the discomfort.

Second, you can be a role model for your child for the best way to handle failure. When you make a mistake, talk to your child about it. Tell them what happened and how you continued and pushed past the initial frustration. Remind them that big feelings aren't the enemy. Instead, we can learn how to control those big feelings and keep moving forward. We shouldn't live life fearing failure. Mistakes are breeding grounds for growth, and perseverance is born when we push through difficult tasks.

## Sins versus Mistakes

Let's take correction a step further. Mistakes are a part of childhood, but so is sin. While both are common, there's a difference between how we should handle a mistake versus how we should handle a sin in our homes. If a child accidentally knocked over his sister's LEGO castle because he didn't see it in the middle of the floor, we probably wouldn't reprimand him. However, if he purposefully went over and smashed it with his fist, we'd address that quite differently. A mistake is an innocent slipup; sin is purposeful, selfish, and rebellious.

No one is exempt from sin. Despite my belief that our identity shouldn't contain the word *sinner*, we are all born sinners. We can't ignore that part of ourselves. If we want to move past it, we must confront our sinful nature.

You may be thinking, *What in the world does sin have to do with self-esteem?* Do you remember what self-esteem is? Confidence in oneself. To truly live the life God laid out for us, we must know who we are in Christ—and part of that is confronting our sinful nature. We can pretend we're perfect and our children never make mistakes, but at some point, our denial will catch up with us. A person who knows their sins are forgiven and who is reconciled with God is better equipped to face this life with confidence.

Kids are sensitive to right versus wrong at a young age. Most two- or three-year-olds immediately start crying when they realize they did something wrong. If we don't confront the wrongdoing early, their sensitivity to sin will start to wane. Then as kids get older, they won't feel as much discomfort or distress when they gossip behind someone's back, hit their brother or sister, or tell a white lie. You may have heard before that "sin is first pleasing, then easy, then delightful, then frequent, and then habitual."[10] Don't let your child's sin become habitual.

Parents, you are your child's covering. Before a child receives the Holy Spirit, who convicts and counsels them, you play that role in their life. Don't be afraid to point out selfish, rebellious behavior when you see it. If there is sin in your home, don't ignore it, confront it. Because if you don't, your kids will pay for it later. The Bible tells us, "For the wages of sin is death" (Rom. 6:23). There are consequences to sin. Wouldn't you rather help your child work through their sinful nature now when they're young instead of later when they experience more of its heartbreaking consequences? A payday will come one day in the future, and you and your child will reap what you sow. Make up your mind now to be paid by God for obedience instead of paying for your sin.

Remember, you want to raise children who thrive in this world. Part of that is teaching your children to fear the Lord and run from evil. We must address sin head-on in our families. Ask God to show you the best way to discipline your children when they purposefully sin. Talk to them about what sin is and give them Bible verses to explain how all of us were born with it. However, don't end the conversation there. Make sure your kids know God is faithful to forgive all of us and to purify us from all unrighteousness (1 John 1:9). Nothing is too bad and no one is too far from God's grace.

## No Longer Slaves to Sin

At the beginning of this section, I said I don't think we should identify as "sinners." It's true we all sin and fall short of the glory of God, but that's not the end of the story. Jesus poured out His own blood and entered the Most Holy Place once and for all so we could obtain eternal redemption. What does this mean? As redeemed children of God, we should expect not to sin anymore. Our old sinful nature left, and we were made new when we accepted Jesus into our hearts. We are new creations because of Jesus.

When we have the Holy Spirit living inside us, each day we should become more and more like Jesus. We are new creations in God. As redeemed children, we should be moving from glory to glory and not be getting tripped up and trapped by the same sins over and over again.

We need to address the sin issue in our children's lives, and how we confront it matters. We should lift them up instead of putting them down. Kids need to know that someone believes in them and sees something worthy of love inside of them. We can't forget that truth when we confront our children's sin. We need to show them the other way to live, meaning we need to tell them about the precious gift of salvation and redemption that Jesus

**Faith Former:** Share and study the following Scripture verses with your family:

> For sin shall not have dominion over you, for you are not under law but under grace. (Rom. 6:14)

> Think carefully about what is right, and stop sinning. (1 Cor. 15:34 NLT)

> Anyone who continues to live in him will not sin. But anyone who keeps on sinning does not know him or understand who he is. (1 John 3:6 NLT)

extends to everyone. Kids and adults need to know that God's love isn't conditional. We don't have to earn it. He can't possibly love us more than He does right now.

As parents, we can extend this same unconditional love to our children. Kids shouldn't have to obey to earn love from their parents. We love them because they are our children. True, there are consequences to disobedience, but a parent's love should never change. And kids need to know this truth.

## Final Thoughts on Self-Esteem

Self-esteem and identity can feel like abstract ideas—we can't see them and they're hard to precisely calculate. But when a person's confidence and self-worth are shaky, you can see the effects of it clearly. Sure, there will be potholes in progress, but you now possess the tools to lay a strong foundation. You have the knowledge to intentionally cultivate your child's thought patterns, habits, and beliefs—leading to a generation of kids who know they're meant for more.

# PART 2

# Setting Your Family Up for Success

# 10

# Homes with Joyful Noise

Every home has an atmosphere. As soon as you step foot through the front door, you can feel it. You can usually tell if there's tension, joy, peace, or frustration in the home. Our spirits want to linger longer in homes that feel safe, secure, and loving. The walls of these homes are alive with laughter, adding warmth to the atmosphere, and we don't want to leave because it feels so good. In this chapter, we'll discover how to create these loving home environments that our spirits crave. The places of refuge where our kids can flourish and form positive neural connections.

## Why We All Need Places of Refuge

I'm writing this chapter days after another horrific shooting at an elementary school. My heart is heavy as I think of the unimaginable pain many families face this week due to the brokenness in our world. Unfortunately, no matter how hard we try to escape the darkness, sometimes we can't. Pain and confusion fill the earth because we inhabit a fallen world. That's all the more reason for us to intentionally create places of refuge at home for our families. We need safe spaces where we can be our true selves and feel fully known, secure, and loved.

As we move through this chapter, you'll see how our home atmosphere connects to our emotional and spiritual health. We can't expect our children to grow emotionally and spiritually if our homes are full of chaos. Hectic homes are incompatible with positive emotional and spiritual health. From a mental health perspective, a calming oasis can bring peace to our stressed-out souls. From a spiritual perspective, healthy homes bring refreshment and peace to our spirits.

Throughout the Bible, we see multiple examples of people needing refreshment. A notable one is found in Psalm 23. Here David talks about God leading him beside still waters and restoring his soul. David even says that when he walks through the dark valleys of death, he isn't afraid. Why? Because he finds comfort and safety in the arms of his heavenly Father. What if our children felt that same sense of peace when they walked out into the dark, scary places?

We can't stop every evil thing from happening in our world, but we can control what's happening inside our homes. We can teach our children to know their true identity and feel secure in who they are so they can walk confidently in all situations like David did. We can create loving home atmospheres where the Bible is taught and lived out daily. We can support the growth of healthy neural connections within them, which leads to emotionally healthy lives.

We spent nine chapters learning how to take every thought captive and win our children's hearts. Now it's time to put these tools into practice. Homelife can either support or hinder emotional and spiritual growth. It's time to examine how the atmosphere of our homes influences our children's brains.

## Parents Set the Tone

A large portion of the tone of the home is established by the parents. Parents, especially mothers, have an opportunity to set the home's atmosphere. Scripture confirms this in Proverbs 21:9:

> It is better to dwell in a corner of the housetop [on the flat oriental roof, exposed to all kinds of weather] than in a house shared with a nagging, quarrelsome, and faultfinding woman. (AMPC)

There's something unique about a woman's ability to create the atmosphere of her home. She can fill it with contention and strife or love, support, and encouragement. Women, we set the tone. Sometimes this responsibility can feel like a burden—one more thing to add to our already overflowing to-do list. Or like an impossible task if homemaking and hospitality don't come naturally to us. I don't want you to see it that way. It's hard work, for sure, but it's also filled with blessing. Homemaking isn't a curse; it's a gift God has given us as women. I remember reading this quote from J. R. Miller years ago, and it's stuck with me ever since:

> Her spirit gives the home its atmosphere. Her hands fashion its beauty. Her heart makes its love. And the end is so worthy, so noble, so divine, that no woman who has been called to be a wife, and has listened to the call, should consider any price too great to pay, to be the light, the joy, the blessing, the inspiration of a home.[1]

Doesn't he make homemaking sound beautiful instead of daunting? What if we could create places our kids want to come home to? Safe havens of refreshment from the rest of the world? Whenever I'm tired and feeling a little emotionally worn from homemaking, I try to remind myself what a privilege it is to set the atmosphere of my home for my children. When I pause, I can make the mindset shift from "Keeping up with the housework is exhausting and not rewarding at all" to "I can give my family a beautiful gift by creating a peaceful home environment."

Wouldn't it be wonderful to create a refuge for our families from the craziness of the broken world? Let's do it!

## Research-Backed Strategies for a Peaceful Home

Let's start by looking at the best methods to boost the mood in our homes. These aren't necessarily tools, like meditation or thought journals. Those activities improve personal growth. The strategies in this chapter focus on enhancing the atmosphere of the home, which has an indirect effect on personal growth. Remember, the goal is to create a positive home environment that supports our children's minds, hearts, and identities.

### 1. An Organized Home

This is a big one, and if I'm being honest, something I'm still working on. While it's a challenge to keep an organized home, I know it's something worth pursuing because disorganized homes add stress to our lives. Studies have shown that clutter has a strong negative impact on our mental health and overall well-being.[2] It makes sense. Our brains become overloaded when we see stuff everywhere. It's part of our design. Our God is a God of order (1 Cor. 14:33), and since we were made in His image, we thrive when there's order in our homes. It brings peace to our brains.

Need more proof? One study looked at the language women used to describe their homes. Using linguistic analysis software, the researchers found that women who described their homes as more stressful had increased depressed mood over the course of the day, whereas women who described their homes as more restorative had decreased depressed mood throughout the day.[3] Our environments impact our minds. Restorative, clean, organized homes positively impact our emotional health.

You may be thinking, *Okay, this sounds great, but how do I actually go about doing this? My life is full, and I often struggle to keep up with the housework. The laundry seems to never end, and it feels like there's never enough time in the day to get everything done.* It's taken two significant shifts in my thinking for me to create an orderly home.

First, if we want a clean home—like a clean mind—we need to prioritize it. My mom used to tell me I wasn't prioritizing housework. I'd get mad and deny it, but when I took a closer look at how I spent my days, I realized she was right. When the kids napped, I'd often choose to scroll through Facebook instead of folding laundry. I'd binge on Netflix instead of straightening up. I'd tell myself, "I need this break. I deserve this break." Then I'd give myself permission to indulge.

The funny part is, right before I expected my husband to get home, I'd get super stressed and frantically start tidying. This also happened in the moments before a friend came over. I'd quickly throw all the unorganized papers and toys into a closet, hoping no one would open the door during the playdate. Moms joke about the last-minute cleanup all the time. It's "normal," right? However, we cannot let life's busyness serve as an excuse to indulge excessively.

Now, I don't want to diminish the importance of self-care. Finding rest isn't just important, it's essential. But we need to find the right balance. We won't necessarily feel like we have the time to tidy, so we need to make the time.

Of course, our homes don't have to be spotless all the time. That's not a realistic goal when living with small kids. But if we know a clutter-free home makes us feel better emotionally and mentally, we must prioritize it. Instead of putting off the cleaning and saying, "It can wait. I'll do it later," we can choose to do it now. Because, let's be honest—later never comes.

Making the switch to tidying instead of scrolling can take time and perseverance. I remember a colleague telling me once that if a task takes only two minutes to do, do it now. Hang in there and remind yourself of all the benefits of having a restorative, organized home. Remembering the "why" will keep you motivated.

The second shift that's helped me create an orderly home is recognizing the truth that I can't do it alone. It shouldn't be one person's responsibility to do all the dishes, laundry, vacuuming, and organizing. Keeping a clean home should be a family affair. If organizing doesn't come naturally to you, ask for help. For the past few months, my aunt has been coming to my house to go through our closets and drawers with me. She's an expert organizer, and her assistance has been a huge blessing. Scheduling it each week keeps me accountable, and I've found that creating designated spaces for all the things keeps the amount of clutter down.

Part of asking for help if you need it is getting your kids involved in the process. You can do this by establishing quick cleanups throughout the day. One cleanup at lunchtime and one ten minutes before the bedtime routine. Set a timer for ten minutes and have everyone take time to tidy. If you have competitive kids like mine, they will be highly motivated by the timer. Our kids love racing the clock and seeing if they can finish cleaning up the playroom before the timer goes off. The tasks often don't take as long as you initially think. Timers can be helpful for adults too. I've already timed myself emptying the dishwasher, and I can do it in under five minutes. If it takes me only a couple of minutes to complete, why do I put off doing it all morning? Seems kind of silly, *right*? The next time you straighten up the living room, set a timer and see how long it really takes. You may be pleasantly surprised.

Home organization doesn't have to feel overwhelming. Yes, the work will never go away, and it won't ever be easy, but you can grow in this area. Your home doesn't have to stay messy forever. If you want to see a change in your home's atmosphere, make tidying a priority—and be sure to ask for help in the process.

## 2. Activating Your Senses the Right Way

Now that your home is tidy, you can start thinking about adding more coziness to it. We'll do this by looking at some of our senses. First, let's unpack what we see. Studies show natural light promotes health and well-being.[4] Sunshine adds warmth to our earth and our souls. It's true that naturally lit homes positively impact our overall mood, but it's unrealistic to think we'll move homes to find better lighting.

Thankfully, there's another option to enjoy the benefits of natural light. If you have a dark home, spend more time outside. In one study, researchers observed that more time spent in outdoor light was associated with fewer depressive symptoms, improved mood, and better sleep quality.[5] Getting outside is good not only for our minds but also for our sleep. All of us could benefit from more outside time. A friend of mine used to tell me, "There's no such thing as bad weather, only bad attire."

Along with natural light, plants and flowers can be mood boosters. I like to think this is true because plant life gives us a glimpse into God's perfect design. When God created the earth, He planned for us to live in the most beautiful garden. It makes sense that gardening and even observing plants or flowers bring peace to our souls. Researchers have found flowers have immediate and long-term impacts on mood, social behaviors, and memory in both males and females.[6] There's something innately calming about observing the beauty of a dahlia, peony, or rose. After reading the research, I started to be more intentional about placing plants and flowers around the house. I love having a flower by my kitchen sink. If I'm feeling stressed washing the sink of dishes, I can pause and observe the beautiful flower God created for me to enjoy.

The second sense we should consider when creating a soothing sanctuary is taste. You may be surprised to learn that our food impacts our mental health. Healthy fats—think coconut and avocado oil—limited fast foods, and larger amounts of fruits and vegetables directly impact inflammatory and neural pathways.[7] Eating the right foods not only helps us physically, but emotionally it leads to improved mood and less stress. We need to pay attention to what we feed our families. Choosing the right foods to keep in our home can make a huge difference in our family's overall health and emotional well-being.

Certainly, I can't bring up the topic of healthy eating without addressing the cost. Over the years, I've heard many people say they can't eat healthy foods because it costs too much money. I wholeheartedly agree—healthy food is more expensive. Healthy meals require money and time. But we can do things to overcome these barriers. For example, we can plant small gardens in our backyards, shop at local farmers markets, and meal plan. All these activities help reduce the cost of food and the stress of eating healthy. Eating this way takes energy, but I'd argue that it's worth it. While often convenient, living off sugar and food dye won't do anything good for our children's brains in the long run.

Another vital sense to consider is sound. Often when our family needs a mental health reset or my kids have a ton of energy and need to center themselves, I turn on worship music. Almost instantly, the mood shifts. Worship music points us back to Jesus and reminds us of God's goodness. Dopamine—a hormone associated with pleasure and feel-good states—is released into the brain when people listen to music they enjoy.[8] Bring peace into your home and turn around crabby moods by playing good music.

## Common Threats to Our Peace

Now that we've looked at everyday practices to bring peace into our homes, it's time to face some of the barriers that threaten our cozy havens.

### 1. A House Filled with Discord

A significant threat to peace is discord and strife in our homes. Of course, none of us want contention in our lives, but it often seems to sneak its way through the front door. One afternoon of sibling arguments or one restless night of sleep is all it takes for crankiness to permeate our homes. Emotional health tends to go on the back burner when that's the case. Forget trying to create healthy thought patterns, we're just trying to make it through the day.

But we can bring peace back into our homes when this happens. To decrease the amount of grumbling and complaining, we need to increase joy and gratitude. How do I know this will do the trick? Because my paternal grandfather lived this well. I can't remember a time when my pappy didn't have a smile on his face. And the thing is, he *definitely* had something to complain and moan about—like the fact that he was partially blind or that his bride could barely speak or walk after suffering a stroke. Yet every time I talked to him, I *always* heard him say, "God is awesome!" He didn't let anything take away his happiness. The joy of the Lord truly was his strength.

His secret was that he didn't just say God was awesome, he lived it. He believed it with all his heart. Even through the tough stuff. Choosing to see the good instead of focusing on the bad is one key to reclaiming peace in our homes.

The second key to protecting the peace of our homes is loving well. Jesus commands us to love the Lord with all our heart, soul, and mind and to love our neighbor as ourselves (Matt. 22:36–39). Jesus knows that when we truly love one another, the fruit of joy manifests in our lives. This is the kind of joy that comes from heaven—joy the world can't take away.

How does this happen exactly? When our hearts are focused on love, fear, strife, and criticism fade away. A critical spirit cannot remain when love overflows in our hearts. Not convinced it's that simple? In the Gospel of John, Jesus talks about abiding in His love and keeping His commandments. Then he says, "These things I have spoken to you, that My joy may remain in you, and that your joy may be full" (John 15:11). When we live in the atmosphere of God's love, His joy bubbles up within us.

Do you want the fruit of joy in your home instead of contention and grief? Start abiding in God's love and practice loving others as yourself. While relaxing worship music and fresh flowers add calmness to the atmosphere, the best thing you'll ever find to bring peace into your home is abiding in Jesus.

### 2. One Bad Moment

Have you ever had one of those terrible, bad moments? I'm sure you have. We all have. On certain days it's hard to love the people in our families. Sometimes our kids do things we don't want them to do, and instead of taking deep breaths, we lose our temper. The atmosphere becomes tense, and we wish we could hit the undo button.

In these situations, we have a choice. We can let that one bad moment ruin the rest of the day, week, or even month or we can choose to hit reset. Check out the list below to find a few ways you can reset the mood of your home after a bad moment:

- *Step back from the tension.* Take a five-minute break during which everyone goes to their rooms for some alone time.
- *Get out of the house.* Often a change in environment can reset the mood and take away the crabbies.
- *Ask for forgiveness.* If you did the exploding on your family, talk to your kids about it and ask for forgiveness. Admit you were wrong and pray as a family, asking God to help the situation.
- *Journal your feelings.* Journaling allows you to get all the bad thoughts out on paper. Kids can do this too. I often ask my children to draw a picture of how they feel when they struggle to articulate it with words. After you get it all out on paper, have a family meeting and talk about what you can do to improve the home's mood.

- *Call a friend.* Sometimes we need to talk and pray through a problem with someone on the outside. Talking to a trusted friend can be helpful, but I must warn you that there may be times it causes more harm than good. Why? Because if we spend the entire time venting and complaining, we focus our attention only on the hardship and start to lose perspective. It's healthy to talk about our feelings and discuss what made us upset, but that shouldn't be our only focus. We should also spend time problem-solving or practicing gratitude for what is going right. Find a balance.

- *Reframe your thoughts.* Write down that one nagging thought that seems to be on repeat. For example, "I'm so tired" or "Everyone is annoying me today" or "The kids keep pushing my buttons." What can you do to reframe those statements to find the good even in the hard? Turn "I'm so tired" into "I'm tired, but I can do something to boost my energy, like take a walk outside or go to bed early tonight."

- *Ask for a break.* About once a week, after my family and I finish dinner, I ask my husband if I can have a few minutes of alone time. I do something to intentionally nourish my emotional health. For example, I take a soothing bath, go for a walk, read a book without distraction, listen to worship music in peace, study my Bible, or journal. I'm more recharged and ready to go after I've had a few minutes to myself. Now, I understand breaks aren't an option for everyone. Some of us parent solo and others have spouses who work long hours or travel often. We may need to get creative to find alone time. This could mean asking a friend to do babysitting swaps or waiting until the kids go to bed at night to find a moment for ourselves. Either way, we should intentionally find time in our schedule to refresh and recharge.

My best advice: do what works for you. For some families, this may look like turning on calming music and lighting a candle while taking a few deep breaths. For other families, it means getting outside and breathing in the fresh air. Experiment, try what works, and keep a journal of the results so you know what to do the next time you need a reset. It may be trial and error, but if you're determined not to let a bad moment ruin your mood, it won't have the power to do so in your family.

### 3. Siblings Who Argue All the Time

Lastly, even the most loving of siblings still have moments of contention. Arguing is inevitable when we spend a lot of time together. It's normal if the constant bickering over who had it first brings down the mood of our homes. Thankfully, we can help our children get along better and reduce the number of quarrels in our homes.

A good way to do this is by teaching our kids how to use I-statements. The I-statement is a specific tool to help children express their feelings using constructive words. Often sibling arguments start because child A does something child B doesn't like, so child A starts yelling at child B. This puts child B on the defensive, making them yell back. We can stop these yelling cycles and improve conflict resolution skills by intentionally teaching I-statements. Here are a few examples:

"I feel _____." Or "I feel _____ when you _____.
    Can you please _____?"

Young children may start with something as simple as "I feel frustrated," while older kids may be able to articulate, "I feel frustrated when you copy everything I'm saying. Can you please stop?"

Before kids learn to use I-statements, they often use you-statements. You-statements look something like this: "You are making me so mad! You are so annoying! You never share with me!"

You-statements put people on the defensive. They feel like an attack instead of an expression of emotion, and no one enjoys being attacked. When you talk to your kids about conflict resolution, ask them how they feel when you give them a sample you-statement. Most kids will respond by saying it makes them feel worse.

Almost every day in our house, I remind my kids to use I-statements. It could be a simple reminder like me saying, "Instead of yelling at your brother, tell him how you feel." Kids may need some initial instruction on the difference between you-statements and I-statements.

Overall, children want to be heard, and it's healthy to get feelings out, but there's a more productive way to do it. That's why it's so wonderful to give kids tools like I-statements. Instead of focusing on the other person's faults, I-statements help kids express how *they* feel. With a bit of teaching and practice, kids can learn to express emotion appropriately and soothe situations instead of exacerbating them. It will not only improve the atmosphere of our homes, but it'll also boost the relationships in our children's lives.

## Work in Progress

While these tips and tools sound wonderful, it's important to note that in our journeys, there will be days when we take five steps forward and two steps backward. Some days I struggle to create a peaceful, patient, and loving home atmosphere. I try my best to implement all the strategies I shared with you, but inevitably life happens, and on occasion, I lose my temper or feel that tightness in my chest again.

Then I'll listen to a podcast or read a blog post about creating moments of deep connection with your kids and how valuable it is to slow down and enjoy life with your family. And pretty soon, I find myself cringing because even though I crave more of that life, I know deep down that's not always my reality.

The tension used to cause me to spiral. I'd think, *I'm a failure as a mom* or *Everyone else has it together but me*. Before I knew it, I'd feel defeated.

Wouldn't it be better if we could use the tension we feel to our advantage instead of fearing we won't get it right? What if the tension helped us grow and stretch?

With time and perspective, I started to see that my self-defeating thoughts did nothing to help me become a better parent. Now, instead of jumping straight to fear and anxiety, I take time to reflect. I honestly ask myself the following questions:

Why do I feel this way?

Is there any bit of truth to what I'm feeling?

Is there something I need to repent of or be courageous enough to change in my life?

If the answer is yes, I give it to God, confess it, and allow Him to work that change in me. If the answer is no, I give myself grace. I tell myself, "Lauren, you're doing the best you can. No one expects you to be a perfect parent. God will show you what to do." Then I may even write down a few things I do well in parenthood to remind myself of my strengths. All of us have strengths and weaknesses. We tend to get into trouble when we start comparing our weaknesses to other people's strengths. Focus on what you do well and make plans to grow in the areas where you could use a little extra help.

When becoming more emotionally healthy, we need to remember that it takes time, and we're all works in progress. We can try our best, but we won't always get it right—and that's okay. If we're going to live this out for a lifetime, we need to give ourselves grace in the process. As long as we submit ourselves to God daily, we can trust Him to fill in the gaps.

## Mission Statements

My hope is that this chapter has prompted you to consider ways in which you can deliberately cultivate grace, love, and order in your home. Now it's time to put the tools you learned into practice. Let's make your dreams a reality by crafting mission statements for your home.

### What Is a Mission Statement?

We need to be intentional when it comes to shaping our homes. Places of refuge don't happen by accident. It's like the famous baseball player Yogi Berra said, "If you don't know where you are going, you might wind up someplace else."[9] That's why we'll spend time crafting a mission statement, which will help you plan where you want to go. Your mission statement will be a declaration of what you want your life to look like, giving you vision and purpose.

### How to Create Your Own Mission Statement

To create a mission statement, first you need to brainstorm. The following questions will help you during your brainstorming session:

What are you called to? What are your current roles? This can be a task, career, ministry, etc.

What gifts, talents, and abilities has God given you?

What do you hope to accomplish this season? This year? In the next five years?

What are your dreams and goals for your home? Your family? Your kids?

What do you want to prioritize in your home life? Examples include rest, organization, fellowship, laughter, etc.

Write down your answers to these questions and ask God to show you the purposes for which He created you. After you think about what you want to achieve, record your mission statement. Under each value, list a few action steps so you can put the dream into practice.

Below you will find an example of a mission statement. This gives you an idea of things you could potentially add to yours. Please be sensitive to God's leading. Your mission will most likely look different than mine. No matter your role, no matter the season, you can give God glory in all that you do. Even if that means you spend most of your day folding laundry or doing dishes.

Now it's your turn. Take a few days to think about your values, hopes, and dreams. Then write out your goals and action steps

 **My Mission Is . . .**

- To create an emotionally healthy home.
  - Sample action steps:
    - ▸ Take an inventory of what we're consuming in the home—TV, books, music—and get rid of anything not bringing life to our spirits.
    - ▸ Practice deep breathing every night before bed.
    - ▸ Learn how to use the cognitive triangle presented in chapter 3 to reframe our thoughts from unhelpful to helpful.
- To raise spiritually thriving children.
  - Sample action steps:
    - ▸ Find time to read and meditate on God's Word daily.
    - ▸ Teach my children how to pray.
    - ▸ Strive to bring God into the everyday moments of life.
- To support my husband and encourage his leadership.
  - Sample action steps:
    - ▸ Pray for my husband daily.
    - ▸ Embrace a gentle and quiet spirit during interactions.
    - ▸ Recognize and thank him when I see him taking spiritual initiative.

- To tenderly love, nurture, and instruct my children.
  - Sample action steps:
    - Find "I love you" moments with each child throughout the day.
    - Teach my kids how to have healthy minds and healed hearts.
    - Strive to be slow to speak and quick to forgive in all interactions.
- Create a home filled with joyful noise.
  - Sample action steps:
    - Play worship music daily.
    - Focus on improving organization and putting quick clean-ups into practice.
    - Find time to laugh with my family daily.
- Find joy in the everyday.
  - Sample action steps:
    - Every morning when I wake up, write down three things I'm thankful for in a journal.
    - Slow down by spending more time outside and less time being distracted by screens.
    - Take time to notice the little things.

in a journal. After you've finished your mission statement, hang it in a place where you'll see it often. That way you can continually remind yourself of your goals and bring your vision to life.

With intention and care, you can set your family up for success. It's no longer a far-off dream. Emotional stability, peace, contentment, and security are within reach. Use this sample mission statement to set up a game plan. Write down the steps to prioritize your family's emotional and spiritual health. Then go and live them out.

# 11

# Rhythms of Rest

I'm not exactly sure when my life of hurry started, but I know I lived it for too many years. In high school, two mornings a week I went to the pool at six and swam for an hour before attending school all day. When I finished my classes, I went back to the pool for an additional two hours before heading home. Then I'd eat dinner, finish my homework, and collapse into bed. The busyness continued in college and graduate school and after I started my first job. Many days I found myself out of the house for almost twelve hours. I got used to living a busy, full life. With my competitive personality, it felt natural and normal to prioritize checking things off my to-do list.

I grew up in an achievement-oriented family. My parents never pressured my siblings and me to excel; it just came naturally. My dad made learning fun. He often gave us math riddles to solve before handing us our after-dinner ice cream. My mom never sat still, and the only time I ever saw her watch TV was when she jumped on her minitrampoline with weights in hand.

My parents never explicitly said, "You need to be productive" or "You need to be doing XYZ," yet as a kid, I noticed they rarely sat still. It's how they grew up. Strong work ethics were part of their families' heritage. Naturally, I picked up the habit too, and soon I started to prioritize work and task completion.

I didn't realize the habit of being busy could actually harm me until I started to experience some gut health issues. I met with a functional doctor, hoping he could boost my health. While he had great suggestions to improve my physical well-being, one of his comments caught me by surprise. He told me, "I think you might be addicted to stress."

At first, I thought, *That can't be.* I didn't feel the classic symptoms of stress. I slept well every night, and I rarely experienced that tight feeling in my chest. Busy schedules and stressful days felt normal to me. I'd been doing it for so many years, and I didn't know any other way. Though as I took the time to self-reflect and dissect my rhythms and routines, I realized he may be right.

Even though my days were filled with good things, I never gave my mind or body a chance to fully rest. My busyness inadvertently worked against my desire to be physically and emotionally healthy. Something had to change.

If I wanted to raise children with balanced brains and whole hearts, I needed to learn how to rest and how to model it for my children. Rest and renewal go hand in hand. Brain renewal is impossible without rest.

## Why Busyness Is a Problem

Around the same time I met with a functional doctor, my husband and I started to read John Mark Comer's *The Ruthless Elimination of Hurry: How to Stay Emotionally Healthy and Spiritually Alive in the Chaos of the Modern World.* If you find yourself addicted to your phone and can't shake the feeling that you're not really living, I highly recommend his book. His words prompted us to completely reevaluate our lives.

We asked ourselves the following questions:

Where are we spending our time?

What are we telling our kids, explicitly and implicitly, about what's important in life?

Are we spending our days fulfilling the mission God called us to or with busyness so we feel productive?

My husband and I hoped to have lives filled with deep meaning, but some of our past choices related to our schedules limited our ability to do so.

Now we have to address the elephant in the room. Is having a strong work ethic a bad thing? You could argue Jesus led a productive, busy life. He got up early, traveled often, and diligently went about His Father's business. We also read that the Proverbs 31 woman woke while it was still night, worked vigorously, and never ate the bread of idleness. If godly people work fervently, why can't we?

The difference between a busy, stressful life and a full, peace-filled life is intention. What is our motivation? Why are we choosing to add specific jobs, tasks, or roles to our lives? To be praised by others? Or to be praised by our Heavenly Father? Our life's focus should always be heavenward. Kingdom work is time-consuming and demanding, but more than that, it's intentional and purposeful. It's not wasteful, and it's not busy for the sake of being busy. This is why we need to pause and reflect. Because when we reflect, we can typically discern if our busyness is from God or our own fleshly desires.

We cannot ignore the negative consequences of a hurried life. Yes, the accolades, awards, and busyness often feel good, but they'll always leave us feeling empty. John Mark Comer describes the consequences of hurry this way:

> Not only does hurry keep us from the love, joy, and peace of the kingdom of God—the very core of what all human beings

crave—but it also keeps us from God *himself* simply by stealing our attention. And with hurry, we always lose more than we gain.[1]

We lose something when we get sucked into hurry. Busyness distracts us from our God-given dreams. And deep down, in the long run, most of us don't want more worldly accolades. We want to hear "well done, good and faithful servant" at the end of our days (Matt. 25:23). When we choose Jesus, we fulfill the purpose for which we were created. Living a spiritually and emotionally healthy life means learning to rest our bodies and our schedules.

## Restful Bodies

Weariness is a natural part of our humanity. Even Jesus grew weary when He walked this earth, because He lived in a physical body like ours, a body that grew tired. We read in John 4:6, "Jacob's well was there; and Jesus, tired from the long walk, sat wearily beside the well about noontime" (NLT).

Jesus's physical body became tired. Even though He was fully divine, His flesh still grew weary. In a way, I find this verse comforting because it shows me Jesus knows what it feels like to be tired from life. He understands what it's like to juggle a million things at once. Jesus knows the struggle is real, and our weariness doesn't surprise Him. I think that's why He modeled rest and gave us direct instructions about it. Most notably, we see that Jesus modeled rest when He slept with a pillow on a boat in the middle of a storm (Mark 4:38). His body needed sleep.

In addition to a physical need for rest, He also modeled a need for spiritual rest. Jesus often practiced rest by pulling away from the crowd and finding solitary places to be alone with God (Mark 1:35; Luke 6:12).

Along with giving us an example, Jesus explicitly talks about weariness. In Matthew 11, Jesus gives specific instructions on finding true rest. Take a moment and let the words of Jesus wash over you. As you read, picture Him speaking directly to your heart.

> Are you tired? Worn out? Burned out on religion? Come to me. Get away with me and you'll recover your life. I'll show you how to take a real rest. Walk with me and work with me—watch how I do it. Learn the unforced rhythms of grace. I won't lay anything heavy or ill-fitting on you. Keep company with me and you'll learn to live freely and lightly. (Matt. 11:28–30 MSG)

Here Jesus offers us another way. A way filled with rest and peace. Right now, He wants us to learn how to sit at His feet and slow down enough to walk with Him. Jesus offers rest to not only our physical bodies but also our spiritual bodies. That's what this chapter is about—learning to create rest in our bodies and in our homes.

## Three Practical Tools to Bring Peace to Your Body

We'll start by discovering three practical ways, besides sleep, to bring physical rest to our bodies. I recently discovered an incredible nerve called the vagus nerve. It's the longest nerve in our bodies and when stimulated, it's designed to bring us rest and relaxation. The vagus nerve is a superhighway that communicates information from our brain to our gut and back from our gut to our brain.

Not only will intentional vagus nerve stimulation help us rest better, but there's even evidence that the vagus nerve suppresses inflammation in the body.[2] By learning to stimulate our vagus nerve, we can start our days with more relaxation, better digestion, and less stress and anxiety. Kids who learn to do this early on will be able to face challenging situations with confidence.

Remember, we can't avoid all stress, but we can learn how to deal with it more effectively.

The following three techniques will help you intentionally stimulate that vagus nerve. The tasks aren't complex, and kids and adults can do them together. We could all benefit from learning how to downregulate our nervous systems and bring rest to our brains and bodies.

### 1. Deep Breathing

Before you get out of bed in the morning and before you fall asleep at night, practice deep breathing. I do this with my kids as part of our bedtime routine. At first, your kids may need instruction on how to take deep belly breaths.

Help them learn to do this by telling them to imagine their stomach as a giant birthday balloon. The balloon starts at the bottom of your ribs and moves down, ending in your hip/pelvic region. As you inhale, picture the belly balloon expanding. Your diaphragm and lower abdomen area should fill with air. As you exhale, imagine the balloon slowly emptying the way a balloon does when you let the air out of it. It's helpful to place your hands around the lower rib area to feel the breath entering your lungs and to feel your diaphragm expanding. You can also gently tie a scarf around the bottom of your ribs. Breathe in for a count of four, hold briefly, then exhale slowly for a count of six. The more you practice deep breathing, the better you will get at it.

Ask your children to share how they feel after you go through a few rounds of deep breathing. See if they notice a difference in their mood. Deep breathing is an excellent tool for kids to learn. They can use it daily or as needed to bring peace to their physical bodies.

### 2. Singing

Singing activates your voice box, which is connected to your vagus nerve. So when you sing, it not only glorifies God but also brings you peace and calm. Something happens physically in our bodies when we sing. How cool is that?

Over and over in the Bible, God commands us to sing. Not only does the atmosphere shift when we praise Jesus, but science now shows that something in our physical bodies shifts as well. As we sing, the vagus nerve sends signals from our central nervous system to the rest of our body to relax. Have you ever noticed how young children sing all the time? They sing as they clean up their toys, put on their shoes, and dance around the living room. Have you also noticed how much more young children smile and giggle compared to adults? I'm telling you, singing does something.

Not only does singing activate relaxation in our bodies, but science now shows we become unified when we sing as a group. Researchers studied choir singers and found that as they performed together, their heartbeats began to synchronize.[3] As the choir members sang in unison, their pulses rose and fell at the same rate.[4] Not only will singing and worship bring a wave of peace to your spirit and your physical body, but they will also unify you with other believers. No wonder God commands us to sing over fifty times in His Word![5] He knew it would activate something powerful within us.

God tells us to sing in the morning, sing to each other, and sing of God's marvelous works. You don't need to have the best voice ever to reap the benefits of singing. Sing with your children and enjoy the biblical and physical benefits.

### 3. Meditation

When I hear the word *meditation*, sometimes I cringe. Why? Because I've seen too many good-intentioned people meditate on the wrong things. We need to be careful about what and who we focus on. Any meditation we listen to online should always point us back to Jesus. Our family loves the Abide app because it has thousands of Christian meditations for children and adults focused on sleep, emotions, healing, and spiritual growth. Not all meditations are created equal. When you choose meditations for your children to listen to before bed or during quiet times, use your Holy Spirit discernment. If it doesn't feel or sound right, turn it off.

Remember what we read in Philippians 4:8? God commands us to meditate on honorable, pure, and wholesome things. Use online meditations to help you and your kids practice intentional peace. When we close our eyes and listen to soothing sounds, the distractions and stress of life melt away. Many people I talk to, both young and old, say meditations help them relax before bed. I often encourage parents with anxious children to try it out and see how it impacts their bodies and brains. My only warning is to use discernment when choosing meditations.

While I've shared three research-backed methods to bring peace to your physical body, of course, other methods exist. As you and your children participate in activities designed to help you relax, pay attention to how your body feels before and after. Discover what activities soothe your soul and find ways to add them into your daily routine.

## Restful Routines

Now it's time to learn how to bring rest to our schedules and homes. Home is where we put everything we've learned into practice. To build restful homes, we can start by taking an inventory of our routines and rhythms.

Adults typically set the routines for the family, so it's worthwhile for parents to take a step back and analyze the tasks and activities that fill their days. That being said, when completing the next activity, feel free to invite your whole family into the process. Your family members may be able to shed light on your family routines. They can also help you find the activities that

**Brain Builder:** Take an inventory of your rest by asking yourself the following questions:

> When I have free time, what do I fill the time with? Does it leave me feeling better or worse than when I started?
>
> What parts of my day feel rushed?
>
> What parts of my day feel restful?
>
> What activities help me and my family thrive?
>
> What activities bring my family stress or dread?
>
> What values do I want to prioritize in my home?

bring the most joy and peace into your lives. Whether you do the brainstorming separately or together, take time to answer the Brain Builder questions above and write down specific examples for each prompt.

Answering these questions will help you determine what matters most in your life. By taking an inventory, you'll also start to clearly see which routines make your soul prosper and which rhythms bring you more stress. As you discover rhythms or routines that need to change, you may be tempted to think, *Our family has been like this for years. How could it possibly be different now?* I've said it before, but it's worth saying again: change takes time.

New rhythms and routines won't magically appear overnight. There will be growing pains, and I wouldn't be surprised if your child rolled her eyes at you a few times in the process. Kids may moan and complain when you change routines, but I encourage you to push past the initial resistance. I love how Rebekah Lyons puts it in *Rhythms of Renewal*: "It's never too late to re-establish what you want your life to be about."[6] You *can* renovate your life to bring you more peace. It's never too late.

## Three Practical Tools to Bring Peace to Your Routine

Now that we've identified our routines and rhythms, we need to figure out how to walk out a restful life. Through research and experience, I've found three tools to help families create rhythms of rest.

### 1. Boundaries with Time

We can't talk about family routines without talking about sports schedules. Sports are a huge part of American culture. When our son turned five, he told us he wanted to play baseball. We looked into the local league and noticed the teams had three to four games scheduled each week. At five years old, that seemed like a big-time commitment. With three small kids at home, I wasn't sure I wanted to be rushing dinner and running somewhere almost every night of the week. It felt like a lot, yet people were doing it.

Every year, across the country, thousands of families sign their five-year-old children up for baseball. Simply because everyone else does a certain thing doesn't mean you should do it too. We decided to wait a few years, and I'm so glad we chose our sanity over sports. Thankfully, when our son played baseball a few years later, the schedule went down to two games per week.

With multiple kids who all have different interests, the family calendar fills up quickly. If we aren't careful with our time, we can find ourselves running to a different field every night of the week. We learned quickly that if we want rhythms of rest, we need to set up boundaries when it comes to extracurricular activities.

We've established two rules in our home regarding outside activities: no sports on Sunday and only one activity per child per season. In truth, the no sports on Sunday hasn't been easy. I didn't like telling my son's soccer coach he would miss all the Sunday games because we had church. I thought they'd judge our family for being too conservative or for being those "weird" Christians. As much as I didn't like feeling different, I knew if we chose to attend the games, our actions would convey to our children that sports are more important than Jesus.

Our routines and rhythms tell our children what we value, sometimes more than our actual words. We can say, "We need to put Jesus first," but if we don't live it out, we lose credibility with our children. Although it was uncomfortable, I'm glad we set the boundary early so our children know where we stand on the issue.

Please hear me, I'm not saying sports are inherently bad. Of course there's value in learning how to play as a team, manage our time, and lose graciously. But I don't want our children to learn these lessons at the expense of their mental sanity or relationship with Jesus. To me, it's not worth it. We've found the best success by praying through each activity. Proverbs 16:9 tells us, "We can make our plans, but the LORD determines our steps" (NLT). Have you prayed and asked God to show you which extracurriculars to invest in? I'm confident God will order your family's steps and show you the best path forward if you bring it to Him in prayer.

Every family's extracurriculars may look different, and that's perfectly normal. Find what works for you and intentionally take time every few months to ask yourself, Is our family thriving in this season? Go back and take the rest inventory again. If your schedule isn't working, be bold enough to admit it. Then learn from the experience and set up more boundaries to protect your rest.

### 2. Learning to Practice Soul Care

Even if we strive to live a simple life, one with limited hurry, we'll all face moments of frustration. Our kids will face them too. No one is exempt from adversity. In these moments of frustration, how do we refresh our minds? The world tells us we need to be better at self-care. Instagram is filled with messages like "Do something for you. You deserve a break. Take a bubble bath, get a massage, go shopping, binge Netflix." Then we won't be so overwhelmed, *right?*

It is certainly okay to treat ourselves every now and then, but do these indulgences bring us the deep nourishment our hearts need? When we chase things of this world, we can fool ourselves into thinking we'll be fulfilled if we just take better vacations or have more toys or buy spacious homes or get slimmer bodies. Both kids and adults deal with the temptation of wanting more stuff or experiences to be happy. The trouble is that these things feed our flesh instead of our souls. The feeling is temporary. We need lasting joy and peace.

What we really crave is connection with our Savior. That's what nourishes our souls. That's how God designed us—to be in communion with Him. Walking intimately with God allows us to find true rest when the world is shaking.

God instructs us in His Ten Commandments to remember the Sabbath and keep it holy (Exod. 20:8). He knew we'd need time away from work to refresh our bodies and souls. Time to find complete rest. In our fast-paced world, purposeful pauses are becoming harder to find. We must be intentional about practicing the Sabbath for our own sakes and for our children's sakes. God wouldn't instruct us to do it and even model it Himself (Exod. 31:17) if it wasn't necessary. If you struggle to take a pause, I highly recommend you study what Scripture has to say about the Sabbath.

At the end of the day, the best way to practice soul care is to go to Jesus. He instructs us to come to Him to find rest (Matt. 11:28). The key word being *come.* We can't find rest if we don't move in action to commune with Him. The deepest form of rest and relaxation you'll experience is at the feet of Jesus.

### 3. Finding Quiet Time

Finally, with active kids at home, how do we find real rest? Mama, I know you're thinking, *This sounds wonderful and nice, but my house is never quiet.* I share the same dilemma, but through the years I've found two strategies to find moments of peace and quiet.

First, set up a quiet-time routine for everyone in your family. Nap time is a treasure, and I urge you not to give it up when your kids stop napping. Set up routines of afternoon rest. Everyone can benefit from taking time to be by themselves. Remember how often Jesus went away from the crowd to be alone and pray? We should follow His example. Research even backs up the benefits of solitude. Amy Morin, psychotherapist and bestselling author, describes the benefits of alone time: "When you carve some solitude into your schedule, you show your children that being alone is healthy. Research shows that kids who learn to be by themselves are better behaved than other children."[7] What parent doesn't want better-behaved kids? Not only that, but having the ability to tolerate alone time is also associated with higher levels of happiness, lower levels of depression, and improved stress management.[8] Emotionally healthy homes make quiet time a priority.

Kids may struggle with quiet time at first, especially if it's a new routine. Be clear about the expectations. Each family may have different rules, but they could sound something like this: "We're all going to take time to slow our brains and rest. This means fifteen minutes of alone time in our rooms. You can read, listen to a book on tape, color, or play quietly. I'll come to get you when quiet time is over." Increase the chances of success by starting with a reasonable amount of time. Then you can slowly increase the amount by five minutes each week until you reach the desired time. Quiet time most likely won't be perfect, and there will be interruptions, but teaching your children how to rest and recharge is a worthwhile endeavor. Their brains will thank you later!

The second way I find some much-needed quiet time for myself is by waking up before my kids and enjoying the quiet house before the day starts. In the past, I used my kids as an alarm clock. I needed sleep and couldn't fathom setting an alarm clock to wake up before 6:30 a.m. Though I soon realized I craved alone time. Time when I could sit and be still. Waking up early is a sacrifice, but it's best for everyone in the long run. When I find time to recharge my spiritual health by waking up early and reading my Bible, I'm a happier mom, which leads to happier kids.

Of course, there have been days when I set my alarm to get up early, and no matter how quietly I tiptoed down the stairs, one of my children heard me and magically appeared by my side. With older kids, you can instruct them to go back to their rooms until the designated wake-up time. My husband and I invested in a "rise to wake clock" when our kids turned three. You can preset the time so the clock turns green when it's time to wake up. Through the years our kids have been great about following the clock and playing quietly in their rooms until it's time to come out. That guarantees me some alone time. Babies can be harder to get back to sleep. If my quiet morning got ruined by a crying baby, I'd take some time to rest during the baby's nap later in the day.

The bottom line is, quiet time won't happen by accident. You must intentionally schedule times of peace and quiet into your day. Life often tempts us to say yes to every opportunity that comes along. Many extracurricular activities are good, but we must be careful not to overbook our family's schedule. Because an overwhelmed schedule leads to an overwhelmed mind.

When we get too busy, there's no time for renewal, breakthrough, or rest—essential ingredients to living an emotionally and spiritually healthy life. We can avoid this by making plans for times of refreshment.

# 12

# A Prayer for You

We started this journey together, seeking ways to nurture our children's spiritual and emotional health. We found practical tools and tasks to help us build deep roots in our children's minds, hearts, and identities. Then we discovered how to walk out the life we crave by creating peaceful home atmospheres and restful rhythms.

As we wrap up our time together, I want you to know one last thing: our journey to spiritual and emotional health won't be linear. Our passage will include bumps, twists, turns, and shifts. One day we'll feel amazing and tell ourselves we're the best parent ever. The next day we'll question every decision we make and feel captivated by fear. In these moments, I want you to march forward and keep your eyes on Jesus. Dearly loved, God chose you. Walk toward Him and clothe yourselves with humility, compassion, gentleness, kindness, and patience (Col. 3:12). By doing that, your parenting will be transformed.

Lastly, don't look to the world to find comfort. God is calling you to peace—to let Christ rule in your heart so His peace can wash over you (v. 15). You are equipped to lay firm foundations in your children's minds, hearts, and identities. You can build your family's house on a solid rock, so when the storms of life come, your family is strong and ready to endure anything.

As we close, I want to declare God's goodness over you in prayer:

*Thank You, Lord, that we are new creations! Thank You that all the old, toxic thought patterns are gone. We still serve a mountain-moving God. As we read, You broke strongholds, healed our hearts, and brought freedom to our souls. Our brains, hearts, and identities have been made new in YOU, and for that we are thankful.*

*God, as we walk forward, order our steps. Help us find the straight and narrow path to walk down with our families and guide our children to find it as well. The world is dark and scary, but as we focus our eyes on You, we trust You will direct us in all things. We put our complete hope in You, the Creator of the heavens and the earth.*

*Lord, thank You for giving us the victory over toxic thoughts, wounds, sins, and lies. In our own strength we may fail, but in You we are victorious! We know there will be bumps in the road of life, and the enemy may even try to throw fiery darts to stop us from living in abundance. The enemy may start something, but God, You have the final say. You are the Name above every other Name, and in You, nothing is impossible.*

*God, watch over these mothers and fathers. I pray that every parent who reads this book knows they are chosen by You. Give them confidence and wisdom to raise emotionally and spiritually healthy kids. Help their children grab hold of their sound minds right now. When faced with two choices, may their kids choose the way of life. As their children go out into the world, keep their feet firmly planted on the solid rock on which You've placed them. In Jesus's name, I pray, amen.*

Tears came to my eyes as I wrote this prayer because I know how hard parenting can be, and many days we feel inadequate or unprepared to lead our children. But God is calling us to a life filled with abundance, and His desire is for every family to live in victory. If life has been hard or parenting has been a struggle, please know this: God can redeem anything. There is nothing He can't fix! He can move that mountain and make that crooked place straight. Seek His face and He will never let you down. You can do this, mama! You can raise God-fearing children who flourish in a broken world.

Now that you're equipped to live the life you've always imagined for your family, go live it.

# Appendix A

# Scripture References for Common Childhood Sins

## Disobedience/Disrespect

If you love Me, keep My commandments. (John 14:15)

But Peter and the other apostles answered and said: "We ought to obey God rather than men." (Acts 5:29)

Children, obey your parents in all things, for this is well pleasing to the Lord. (Col. 3:20)

For men will be lovers of themselves, lovers of money, boasters, proud, blasphemers, disobedient to parents, unthankful, unholy. (2 Tim. 3:2)

## Lying

Then keep your tongue from speaking evil
and your lips from telling lies! (Ps. 34:13 NLT)

Lying lips are an abomination to the LORD,
But those who deal truthfully are His delight. (Prov. 12:22)

For the Scriptures say,
"If you want to enjoy life
and see many happy days,
keep your tongue from speaking evil
and your lips from telling lies.
Turn away from evil and do good.
Search for peace, and work to maintain it. (1 Pet.
3:10–11 NLT)

## Selfishness

But he will pour out his anger and wrath on those who live for themselves, who refuse to obey the truth and instead live lives of wickedness. (Rom. 2:8 NLT)

For wherever there is jealousy and selfish ambition, there you will find disorder and evil of every kind. (James 3:16 NLT)

If someone has enough money to live well and sees a brother or sister in need but shows no compassion—how can God's love be in that person? (1 John 3:17 NLT)

## Teasing/Being Cruel

The tongue can bring death or life;
those who love to talk will reap the consequences.
(Prov. 18:21 NLT)

A fool vents all his feelings,
But a wise man holds them back. (Prov. 29:11)

Let no corrupt word proceed out of your mouth, but what is good for necessary edification, that it may impart grace to the hearers. (Eph. 4:29)

Obscene stories, foolish talk, and coarse jokes—these are not for you. Instead, let there be thankfulness to God. (Eph. 5:4 NLT)

## Stealing

You must not steal. (Exod. 20:15 NLT)

Do not steal. Do not deceive or cheat one another. (Lev. 19:11 NLT)

If you are a thief, quit stealing. Instead, use your hands for good hard work, and then give generously to others in need. (Eph. 4:28 NLT)

## Appendix B

# Scripture References for Understanding Our God-Given Identities

So God created man in His own image; in the image of God He created him; male and female He created them. (Gen. 1:27)

> Your eyes saw my substance, being yet unformed.
> And in Your book they all were written,
> The days fashioned for me,
> When as yet there were none of them. (Ps. 139:16)

For God so loved the world that He gave His only begotten Son, that whoever believes in Him should not perish but have everlasting life. (John 3:16)

Knowing this, that our old man was crucified with Him, that the body of sin might be done away with, that we should no longer be slaves of sin. (Rom. 6:6)

Yet in all these things we are more than conquerors through Him who loved us. (Rom. 8:37)

But of Him you are in Christ Jesus, who became for us wisdom from God—and righteousness and sanctification and redemption. (1 Cor. 1:30)

For "who has known the mind of the LORD that he may instruct Him?" But we have the mind of Christ. (1 Cor. 2:16)

Therefore, if anyone is in Christ, he is a new creation; old things have passed away; behold, all things have become new. (2 Cor. 5:17)

I have been crucified with Christ; it is no longer I who live, but Christ lives in me; and the life which I now live in the flesh I live by faith in the Son of God, who loved me and gave Himself for me. (Gal. 2:20)

Therefore you are no longer a slave but a son, and if a son, then an heir of God through Christ. (Gal. 4:7)

Blessed be the God and Father of our Lord Jesus Christ, who has blessed us with every spiritual blessing in the heavenly places in Christ. (Eph. 1:3)

And raised us up together, and made us sit together in the heavenly places in Christ Jesus. (Eph. 2:6)

For we are His workmanship, created in Christ Jesus for good works, which God prepared beforehand that we should walk in them. (Eph. 2:10)

And that you put on the new man which was created according to God, in true righteousness and holiness. (Eph. 4:24)

For our citizenship is in heaven, from which we also eagerly wait for the Savior, the Lord Jesus Christ. (Phil. 3:20)

For God has not given us a spirit of fear, but of power and of love and of a sound mind. (2 Tim. 1:7)

Who has saved us and called us with a holy calling, not according to our works, but according to His own purpose and grace which was given to us in Christ Jesus before time began. (2 Tim. 1:9)

But you are a chosen generation, a royal priesthood, a holy nation, His own special people, that you may proclaim the praises of Him who called you out of darkness into His marvelous light. (1 Pet. 2:9)

But the anointing which you have received from Him abides in you, and you do not need that anyone teach you; but as the same anointing teaches you concerning all things, and is true, and is not a lie, and just as it has taught you, you will abide in Him. (1 John 2:27)

You are of God, little children, and have overcome them, because He who is in you is greater than he who is in the world. (1 John 4:4)

# Acknowledgments

God placed a desire in my heart five years ago to write a book, and to see it come to life has been incredibly challenging yet rewarding. It feels like I just birthed my fourth child! The privilege of sharing my words with the world is not lost on me. None of this would have been possible without the support and help of others.

First and foremost, I want to thank God for sustaining me through the last year and literally bending time to make space in my schedule to write. Thank You for bringing the book to completion. You are always faithful to finish what You start. I love you, Jesus.

Next up is my loving husband, Darryl, who so graciously gave me extra time and space to lock myself in our prayer room and write. The nature of your job is demanding, yet you never let that stop you from taking on extra household duties. Thank you! Along with that, your daily prayers mean more to me than you will ever know. I'm forever grateful God brought us together. It's easy to follow a man who so diligently follows Jesus.

Brian Vos, my acquiring editor, thank you for believing in my vision and taking a chance on me. You championed this book from the beginning and have helped me carefully refine it into gold. Working with you has been an absolute pleasure. To the rest of Team Baker and the entire marketing team, thank you for partnering with me and helping the world find and connect with the words inside this book.

To Kyle Negrete, thank you for believing in me and casting a vision that was far greater than anything I could have imagined. I truly appreciate you.

Thank you to Danielle Hale and the rest of the Fedd Agency team for always cheering me on and believing in my dreams. I'm so grateful for your support, and I could not have done this without you!

To Mom and Dad, you've had my back since birth. Your unconditional love and support have changed my life for the better, and seriously, this book would not be here if it weren't for you. Thank you for always offering a helping hand and praying over this thing from the beginning.

To the best in-laws a girl could ask for, Dave and Elaine, thank you for talking through many of these chapters with me. You are always patient with me, yet you push me to be better. Thank you from the bottom of my heart.

To my incredible children, Ellie, Isaiah, and Adelyn. My greatest pleasure in life is being your mom. You constantly bring a smile to my face, and I'm so grateful God entrusted me with three beautiful gifts. Thank you for allowing Mommy to step away from time to time and never (okay, rarely) complaining about me taking time to write.

To my sister and best friend, Kate Santana. Our voice texts bring me life and I truly appreciate everything you've done to make this book possible. From offering your feedback to watching my kids, I'm blessed to have you as my sister.

My dear Nona, who knows how to make anyone feel like a million bucks, thank you for laying a firm foundation of faith in my life at a young age. You and Pop-Pop have started a legacy of faith and love, and I pray it continues for generations to come!

This book would not be what it is today without the help and support of my friend Jill McCormick. Thank you for encouraging me to dig deeper and always providing honest, loving feedback about the words I wrote.

I also want to thank Christy Boulware, Erika Butler, Christina Hibbs, and Angie Wakeman for encouraging me in the ups and downs of the writing process. Your prayers sustained me, and I'm grateful you are in my life!

I can't forget my aunt Kara Young for coming to tidy my house as I neglected organization to write instead. Your support through the years has meant so much to me.

I also want to thank Lysa TerKeurst, Ruth Schwenk, and the team at COMPEL Training for taking a chance on me and teaching me how to write a book through your book proposal boot camp. Your feedback shaped me as a writer, and I'm thankful I had the opportunity to sit under you for a few months and learn from the best.

To my church family, friends, and extended family who have offered support and encouragement in this process. Thank you for encouraging me in my walk and believing in the dreams God has given me.

Jesus, after Adelyn was born the first words out of my mouth were "Jesus, we did it! We did it!" as tears rolled down my face. Again, tears fill my eyes as I type, "Jesus, we did it!"

# About Inspired Motherhood

As you learn how to lay a solid foundation in your children's lives, it is great to connect with other like-minded families. That's why inspired-motherhood.com is the place for you!

At Inspired Motherhood, moms are empowered to know their worth, and families are equipped with the tools to raise spiritually and emotionally healthy kids. You'll learn how to cultivate deep roots in your children and create sacred spaces where your family can thrive. Come be refreshed, renewed, and equipped to raise up the next generation in courage and love.

Join our community today at www.inspired-motherhood.com.

# Notes

## Chapter 1 The Mental Game of Motherhood

1. Jennie Allen, *Get Out of Your Head: Stopping the Spiral of Toxic Thoughts* (Colorado Springs: WaterBrook, 2020), 42.

2. Jack W. Hayford, ed., *New Spirit-Filled Life Bible NKJV* (Nashville: Thomas Nelson, 2002), 1569.

## Chapter 2 The Three Key Growth Areas

1. Lund University, "Babies Know When You Imitate Them—and Like It," ScienceDaily, May 26, 2020, www.sciencedaily.com/releases/2020/05/200526111251.htm.

2. "Brain Architecture," Center on the Developing Child at Harvard University, March 19, 2015, https://developingchild.harvard.edu/science/key-concepts/brain-architecture/.

3. C. Lebel et al., "Microstructural Maturation of the Human Brain from Childhood to Adulthood," *Neuroimage* 40, no. 3 (January 2008): 1044–55, https://pubmed.ncbi.nlm.nih.gov/18295509/.

4. Judith S. Beck, *Cognitive Behavior Therapy: Basics and Beyond* (New York: Guilford Press, 2021), 232.

5. "Research Shows That Spiritual Maturity Process Should Start at a Young Age," Barna, November 17, 2003, https://www.barna.com/research/research-shows-that-spiritual-maturity-process-should-start-at-a-young-age/.

6. "Research Shows."

7. Dario Cvencek, Anthony G. Greenwald, and Andrew N. Meltzoff, "Implicit Measures for Preschool Children Confirm Self-Esteem's Role in Maintaining a Balanced Identity," *Journal of Experimental Social Psychology* 62 (January 2016): 50–57, https://www.sciencedirect.com/science/article/abs/pii/S0022103115001250.

8. "Brain Architecture."

9. "Brain Architecture."

## Chapter 3 Your Thoughts Have Power

1. Henry M. Wellman et al., "Early Understanding of Emotion: Evidence from Natural Language," *Cognition and Emotion* 9, no. 2/3 (1995): 117–49, https://www.tandfonline.com/doi/abs/10.1080/02699939508409005.

2. Andrew B. Newberg and Mark Robert Waldman, *Words Can Change Your Brain: 12 Conversation Strategies to Build Trust, Resolve Conflict, and Increase Intimacy* (New York: Penguin, 2012), 24.

3. Jackie Lodge, Diana Kim Harte, and Gail Tripp, "Children's Self-Talk Under Conditions of Mild Anxiety," *Journal of Anxiety Disorders* 12, no. 2 (1998): 153–76, https://www.sciencedirect.com/science/article/abs/pii/S0887618598000061?via%3Dihub.

4. Mayo Clinic Staff, "Positive Thinking: Stop Negative Self-Talk to Reduce Stress," Mayo Clinic, February 3, 2022, https://www.mayoclinic.org/healthy-lifestyle/stress-management/in-depth/positive-thinking/art-20043950.

5. Newberg and Waldman, *Words Can Change Your Brain*, 35.

6. Amy Morin, "5 Exercises That Train Your Brain for Happiness and Success," *Psychology Today*, March 21, 2017, https://www.psychologytoday.com/us/blog/what-mentally-strong-people-dont-do/201703/5-exercises-train-your-brain-happiness-and-success.

7. Dr. Caroline Leaf, *Switch On Your Brain: The Key to Peak Happiness, Thinking, and Health* (Grand Rapids: Baker Books, 2015), 24.

## Chapter 4 Overcoming the Most Common Mental Mistakes

1. Martin E. P. Seligman, Tayyab Rashid, and Acacia C. Parks, "Positive Psychotherapy," *American Psychologist Pennsylvania* (November 2006): 776, https://ppc.sas.upenn.edu/sites/default/files/positivepsychotherapyarticle.pdf.

2. J. Kim Penberthy, "What Science Tells Us about How to Overcome Regret," World Economic Forum, January 12, 2022, https://www.weforum.org/agenda/2022/01/neurobehavioral-scientist-shows-how-people-can-overcome-regret-mental-health/.

3. Eva Ose Askvik, F. R. (Ruud) van der Weel, and Audrey L. H. van der Meer, "The Importance of Cursive Handwriting over Typewriting for Learning in the Classroom: A High-Density EEG Study of 12-Year-Old Children and Young Adults," *Frontiers in Psychology* 11 (2020): 1–16, https://www.frontiersin.org/articles/10.3389/fpsyg.2020.01810/full.

4. Askvik, van der Weel, and van der Meer, "The Importance of Cursive Handwriting."

## Chapter 5 The Guard over Your Garden

1. James Strong, *The New Strong Expanded Exhaustive Concordance of the Bible* (Nashville: Thomas Nelson, 2001), 190.
2. Strong, *The New Strong Expanded*, 139.
3. Donald C. Stamps and J. W. Adams, *The Full Life Study Bible: King James Version* (Grand Rapids: Zondervan, 1992), 1494.
4. Strong, *The New Strong Expanded*, 267.
5. Stamps and Adams, *The Full Life Study Bible*, 1868.
6. Hayford, *New Spirit-Filled Life Bible NKJV*, 1566.

## Chapter 6 Our Walls Have Scars

1. Hayford, *New Spirit-Filled Life Bible NKJV*, 701–2.

## Chapter 7 Winning Your Child's Heart

1. J. Ronald Lally and Peter L. Mangione, "Caring Relationships: The Heart of Early Brain Development," *Young Children* 72, no. 2 (May 2017), https://www.naeyc.org/resources/pubs/yc/may2017/caring-relationships-heart-early-brain-development.
2. Laura E. Berk, *Development through the Lifespan* (Boston: Pearson, 2018), 205.
3. Patricia A. Thomas, Hui Liu, and Debra Umberson, "Family Relationships and Well-Being," *Innovation in Aging* 1, no. 3 (November 2017): 1–11, https://doi.org/10.1093/geroni/igx025.
4. Ann Mastergeorge et al., *Understanding Family Engagement Outcomes: Research to Practice Series, Positive Parent-Child Relationships* (National Center on Parent, Family, and Community Engagement, 2013), http://www.foursquarecommunityactioninc.com/Documents/Parent_Child_Relationships.pdf.
5. "Opportunities for Faith Formation at Home," Barna, April 21, 2020, https://www.barna.com/faith-formation-at-home/.
6. "Opportunities for Faith Formation at Home."
7. Marla E. Eisenberg et al., "Correlations between Family Meals and Psychosocial Well-being among Adolescents," *Archives of Pediatric and Adolescent Medicine* 158, no. 8 (2004): 792–96, doi:10.1001/archpedi.158.8.792.
8. Jeff Thompson, "Is Nonverbal Communication a Numbers Game?," *Psychology Today*, September 30, 2011, https://www.psychologytoday.com/us/blog/beyond-words/201109/is-nonverbal-communication-numbers-game.
9. Berk, *Development through the Lifespan*, 282.
10. Lea Bornstein and Marc H. Bornstein, "Parenting Styles and Child Social Development," Encyclopedia on Early Childhood Development, January 10, 2007, http://citeseerx.ist.psu.edu/viewdoc/download?doi=10.1.1.528.635&rep=rep1&type=pdf.
11. Berk, *Development through the Lifespan*, 284.

## Chapter 8 Our Identity as Children of God

1. "My Child's Tooth Is Turning Dark," Sydney Paediatric Dentistry, accessed September 21, 2022, https://sydneypaediatricdentistry.com/my-childs-tooth-is-turning-dark/.

2. Matt Webel, "Daniel 1: Know Your Name–Claiming Our Identity," sermon, Highrock Haverhill, January 6, 2019, https://www.highrockhaverhill.org/sermon/daniel-1-know-your-name-claiming-our-identity.

## Chapter 9 Building Your Child's Self-Esteem

1. "Self-Esteem: What Is It?," University of Maryland Department of Sociology, accessed September 21, 2022, https://socy.umd.edu/about-us/self-esteem-what-it.

2. Berk, *Development through the Lifespan*, 260.

3. Dario Cvencek, Anthony G. Greenwalk, and Andrew N. Meltzoff, "Implicit Measures for Preschool Children Confirm Self-Esteem's Role in Maintaining a Balanced Identity," *Journal of Experimental Social Psychology* 62 (January 2016): 50–57, https://www.sciencedirect.com/science/article/abs/pii/S0022103115001250.

4. Renee D. Goodwin et al., "Trends in Anxiety among Adults in the United States, 2008–2018: Rapid Increases among Young Adults," *Journal of Psychiatric Research,* August 21, 2020, https://www.ncbi.nlm.nih.gov/pmc/articles/PMC7441973/.

5. Stamps and Adams, *The Full Life Study Bible*, 1105.

6. Paul C. Burnett, "Self-Talk in Upper Elementary School Children: Its Relationship with Irrational Beliefs, Self-Esteem, and Depression," *Journal of Rational-Emotive and Cognitive-Behavior Therapy*, September 1994, https://link.springer.com/article/10.1007/BF02354595.

7. Claudia M. Mueller and Carol S. Dweck, "Praise for Intelligence Can Undermine Children's Motivation and Performance," *Journal of Personality and Social Psychology* 75, no. 1 (1998): 33–52, https://doi.org/10.1037/0022-3514.75.1.33.

8. Mueller and Dweck, "Praise for Intelligence."

9. Eddie Brummelman, Jennifer Crocker, and Brad J. Bushman, "The Praise Paradox: When and Why Praise Backfires in Children with Low Self-Esteem," *Child Development Perspectives* 10, no. 2 (March 2016): 111–15, https://pure.uva.nl/ws/files/13833921/The_Praise_Paradox.pdf.

10. Hayford, *New Spirit-Filled Life Bible NKJV*, 1559.

## Chapter 10 Homes with Joyful Noise

1. J. R. Miller, *Secrets of a Happy Home Life* (Bristol, UK: White Tree Publishing, 2018), 10.

2. Catherine A. Roster, Joseph R. Ferrari, and M. Peter Jurkat, "The Dark Side of Home: Assessing Possession 'Clutter' on Subjective Well-Being," *Journal*

*of Environmental Psychology* 46 ( June 2016): 32–41, https://www.sciencedirect
.com/science/article/abs/pii/S0272494416300159?via%3Dihub.

3. Darbe E. Saxbe and Rena Repetti, "No Place Like Home: Home Tours
Correlate with Daily Patterns of Mood and Cortisol," *Personality and Social
Psychology Bulletin* 36, no. 1 ( January 2010): 71–81, https://doi.org/10.1177
/0146167209352864.

4. Mohamed Boubekri et al., "Impact of Windows and Daylight Exposure
on Overall Health and Sleep Quality of Office Workers: A Case-Control Pilot
Study," *Journal of Clinical Sleep Medicine* 10, no. 6 ( June 2014): 603–11, https://
doi.org/10.5664/jcsm.3780.

5. Angus C. Burns et al., "Time Spent in Outdoor Light Is Associated with
Mood, Sleep, and Circadian Rhythm-Related Outcomes: A Cross-Sectional
and Longitudinal Study in over 400,000 UK Biobank Participants," *Journal of
Affective Disorders* 295 (December 2021): 347–52, https://www.sciencedirect
.com/science/article/pii/S0165032721008612.

6. Jeannette Haviland-Jones et al., "An Environmental Approach to Positive
Emotion: Flowers," *Evolutionary Psychology* 3, no. 1 ( January 2005), https://
doi.org/10.1177/147470490500300109.

7. Joseph Firth et al., "Food and Mood: How Do Diet and Nutrition Affect
Mental Wellbeing?," *BMJ* ( June 2020), https://www.bmj.com/content/369
/bmj.m2382.

8. Sonya McGilchrist, "Music 'Releases Mood-Enhancing Chemical in
the Brain,'" BBC News, January 9, 2011, https://www.bbc.com/news/health
-12135590.

9. Houston Mitchell, "Yogi Berra Dies at 90: Here Are Some of His Greatest Quotes," *Los Angeles Times*, May 12, 2015, https://www.latimes.com/sports
/sportsnow/la-sp-sn-yogi-berra-turns-90-quotes-20150512-story.html.

## Chapter 11 Rhythms of Rest

1. John Mark Comer, *The Ruthless Elimination of Hurry: How to Stay Emotionally Healthy and Spiritually Alive in the Chaos of the Modern World* (Colorado
Springs: Waterbrook, 2019), 25.

2. Roderik J. S. Gerritsen and Guido P. H. Band, "Breath of Life: The Respi-
ratory Vagal Stimulation Model of Contemplative Activity," *Frontiers in Human
Neuroscience* (October 2018), https://www.ncbi.nlm.nih.gov/pmc/articles/PMC
6189422/.

3. Rebecca Morelle, "Choir Singers 'Synchronise Their Heartbeats,'" BBC
News, July 9, 2013, https://www.bbc.com/news/science-environment-23230411.

4. Morelle, "Choir Singers."

5. Bob Kauflin, "Words of Wonder: What Happens When We Sing?," Desir-
ing God, September 27, 2008, https://www.desiringgod.org/messages/words
-of-wonder-what-happens-when-we-sing.

6. Rebekah Lyons, *Rhythms of Renewal: Trading Stress and Anxiety for a Life
of Peace and Purpose* (Grand Rapids: Zondervan, 2019), 31.

7. Amy Morin, "7 Science-Backed Reasons You Should Spend More Time Alone," *Psychology Today*, August 5, 2017, https://www.psychologytoday.com /us/blog/what-mentally-strong-people-dont-do/201708/7-science-backed -reasons-you-should-spend-more-time.

8. Morin, "7 Science-Backed Reasons."

**Lauren Gaines** is an author, writer, teacher, and mother. She is the creator of Inspired Motherhood, a thriving online community for moms to find practical tools to raise spiritually and emotionally healthy kids. Lauren has a unique take on parenting, as she's a busy mom of three children and holds a master's degree in school psychology. Because of her experience teaching as an adjunct professor of psychology, she deeply understands the mental overload families experience. Lauren is married to Darryl, and they live in Bethlehem, Pennsylvania, with their three kids.

Connect with Lauren:

 @inspiredmotherhoodhome

 @inspired.motherhood

 @inspiredmomblog